CW00868211

TWO VOICES

Ego and Spirit

Nickolas Martin, Ed. D.
and
Linda M. Martin, Mh. D.

BALBOA.
PRESS

A DIVISION OF HAY HOUSE

Copyright © 2014 Nickolas Martin, Ed. D. and Linda M. Martin, Mh. D.

All rights reserved. No part of this book may be used or reproduced by any means, graphic, electronic, or mechanical, including photocopying, recording, taping or by any information storage retrieval system without the written permission of the publisher except in the case of brief quotations embodied in critical articles and reviews.

Balboa Press books may be ordered through booksellers or by contacting:

Balboa Press
A Division of Hay House
1663 Liberty Drive
Bloomington, IN 47403
www.balboapress.com
1 (877) 407-4847

Because of the dynamic nature of the Internet, any web addresses or links contained in this book may have changed since publication and may no longer be valid. The views expressed in this work are solely those of the authors and do not necessarily reflect the views of the publisher, and the publisher hereby disclaims any responsibility for them.

The authors of this book do not dispense medical advice or prescribe the use of any technique as a form of treatment for physical, emotional, or medical problems without the advice of a physician, either directly or indirectly. The intent of the authors is only to offer information of a general nature to help you in your quest for emotional and spiritual well-being. In the event you use any of the information in this book for yourself, which is your constitutional right, the authors and the publisher assume no responsibility for your actions.

Any people depicted in stock imagery provided by Thinkstock are models, and such images are being used for illustrative purposes only.
Certain stock imagery © Thinkstock.

Printed in the United States of America.

ISBN: 978-1-4525-9283-1 (sc)
ISBN: 978-1-4525-9282-4 (hc)
ISBN: 978-1-4525-9281-7 (e)

Library of Congress Control Number: 2014903265

Balboa Press rev. date: 03/14/2014

CONTENTS

CHAPTER 3

CHAPTER 4

CHAPTER 5

CHAPTER 6

PREFACE

You, we, and everyone have two "voices" that speak to us from within. Each represents an energy at work in our life. They are the constituents of our soul and define the "you" of our being—the distinctive you that can only be, well, you. The unique you, unlike anyone who ever has or ever will live, yet similar to and connected to everyone who has ever lived. One voice is human, and the other is Divine. These voices, the voices of Ego and Spirit, have resided in everyone who ever has or ever will live a human life.

The one we "listen" to, but often do not recognize and have not awakened to, constantly and profoundly impacts our lives for better or worse. This is the voice we are living, and the foundation for the version of ourselves that we are presenting to the world. For the greater portion of most of our lives, this voice is ego, particularly if we have not awakened spiritually. Our ego unconsciously operates outside of our awareness as the default mode we live in until we have awakened egoically, spiritually, or both.

The vast majority of people live—or more accurately, exist—on an egoically and spiritually unconscious level. This includes many religious followers who have confused religiosity with spirituality. This confusion often stresses intolerance and exclusion rather than understanding and inclusion. Most of our planet is asleep, in an egoically unconscious slumber that contributes to the suffering Buddha was referring to and the destructiveness seen both individually and collectively in our world. This destructiveness takes root in the ego's efforts to help us in our daily and mortal survival, both individually and collectively. These efforts to survive often stress getting more and more of what surrounds us while neglecting more and more of what is within us. This unconscious egoic slumber also precludes the possibility of humankind ever truly knowing world peace.

Most of the effort to awaken us over the past three thousand years has focused on awakening us spiritually while neglecting egoic awakening. This effort does attempt to awaken us to more of what is available within us. Unfortunately, our planet will continue to remain asleep if the only voice that people are attempting to hear, and the only energy they are getting to know, is that of their Spirit. People have only been attempting to awaken to their Divinity, while failing to fully awaken to the core essence of their humanity — their ego. The loud but unrecognized voice of ego will drown out much of what Spirit is attempting to share about itself and its presence in one's being. Spirit therefore remains a voice in the wilderness of one's life, left largely unheard. This also prevents people from hearing the spiritual voice of others. Many wonderful sentiments about God, life, and humanity thus remain unable to penetrate the egoic wall of unconsciousness for very long, if at all. That's why after attending religious services, people so often return to the issues of power, flexibility, or vulnerability playing out in their daily lives, which may involve work, relationships, achievement, health, and so on. For some, a spiritual "honeymoon" occurs, lasting only until the next significant life challenge that inevitably occurs. This challenge pulls them back into the survival focus that often remains at work in the realm of the unconscious ego, and back to a deafness to the voice of their Spirit.

You may be asking several important questions, to which we will respond in turn, such as, "Why can't I hear these voices, and what does it mean to hear them?", "Can these voices hear each other?", "How do I know when I am hearing them?", "Why do I need to hear them?", "Do I need to hear both of them?", "What will happen when I begin to hear them?", "Do I have a voice?", "What do you mean by power, flexibility, and vulnerability issues?", "What do you mean by spiritual unconsciousness?", and "Is a higher level of spiritual consciousness available to everyone?"

Why can't I hear these voices, and what does it mean to hear them?

The voices of Ego and Spirit are inner voices. They do not use sounds or words in the way we are accustomed to hearing voices. We become attuned to them by listening to the way they are speaking within the life we are living. They are speaking within the thoughts, beliefs, behaviors, emotions, and physiology we are experiencing. These are the clues and cues to the nature of the distinctive energies at work in our being. You can learn to hear them, just not in the way you might expect to hear them. One of the purposes of this book is to help you hear them by putting what they would tell you into words if they had a literal voice. We also aim to point out how they are talking to you in your thoughts, behaviors, and emotions, using examples that directly reflect the power, flexibility, and vulnerability issues that make it difficult to hear one's egoic voice as well as the voice of one's Spirit.

Can these voices hear each other?

The voice of Ego is not able to hear Spirit's voice. It operates as if it were the only energy available to you that holds the paramount goal of your daily and mortal survival. If you are experiencing significant issues in the power, flexibility, or vulnerability of your ego, your ego is speaking loudly and you are listening very intensely to the voice of your ego, which means you are living your egoic voice. Though you do not realize you are doing this. Egoic unconsciousness is occurring, and egoic energy is drowning out the voice of Spirit. Ego doesn't do this "on purpose," as it doesn't know who you are, who God is, or even what it is. Ego has no awareness of itself, but it exerts a tremendous impact upon your life. Again, the "words" of ego and the examples that we will be providing are simply intended to bring greater clarity regarding egoic issues of power, flexibility, and vulnerability, as most of this information is likely to be new to you.

In actuality, it doesn't matter whether Ego can hear the voice of Spirit. What matters is that *you* are able to do so. This makes Divine Energy available to you in the transformative process of becoming You. What also matters is that you begin to use your "voice" to speak to ego through your ego awareness and reality-based thinking which we refer to as *mental medicine*. This brings your egoic energy into balance while allowing you to experience the best of your humanity. What makes this possible is your ability to reflect upon your consciousness, to think about your thinking, and to know the difference between belief and truth, if you want to. You can become the owner of your mind, rather than allowing Ego to maintain this ownership in its exaggerated efforts to help you survive, which often lead to suffering. We can each create the person we want to be. This is one of the Four Great Gifts we have been given to create life — *our* life. We only need to understand the energies of a human and Divine nature to do so. One is perfect just the way it is, and the other, we can transform.

The voice of Spirit cannot hear Ego's voice, and it does not need to hear it. Spirit "hears" Ego's voice within the way you are living your life. Spirit is Divine Energy, meaning it is not impacted and cannot be impacted by egoic energy. It does not need to change or be transformed because it is perfect the way it is, and it is always available to you. Furthermore, Divine Energy impacts you and does not directly impact ego. It only exerts indirect impact on Ego. While working in tandem with your efforts to transform and heal your ego, your ego can "learn" that the energy it puts into your survival can be channeled into healthier human experiences and the absence of suffering. This transformation rests upon your ability to recognize human truth and Divine Truth.

How do I know when I am hearing the voices of Ego and Spirit?

These voices speak to us in several key areas of life, and we can tune in to what they are "saying" within these realms. Some of the most important and consistent areas in which we hear Ego and Spirit include how we interact with people in general; the way we act with loved ones; the way we are with ourselves; how we go about using our potential; our ability to work with and grow our mind where needed; how we deal with the significant changes, adversity, stressors, and conflicts that inevitably occur in our lives; and the kinds of emotions we often feel. These are the places where unrecognized healthy and unhealthy patterns in our thoughts, behaviors, emotions, and physiology are being manifested. The greater your difficulty or suffering in any or many of these realms of life, the louder the voice of your ego, and the more you have been listening to it. Again, this holds true even if you do not realize it is happening.

Why do I need to hear these voices?

A failure to hear these voices will cause you to miss much of what is happening in your life and much of what could happen to make your life better. Most people are settling for less out of life and themselves rather than more. It's not their fault. They are all fundamentally good, intelligent, and well-meaning people. To be sure, most people experience happy moments and good times. However, these good periods of time are often separated by longer periods of quiet desperation, in which people wait for something or someone good to happen to them. People often try to shorten these periods with pseudo-happiness, emphasizing entertainment (often mindless), possessions, drugs, or alcohol, just to name a few, rather than natural, healthy experiences that are priceless, can't be bought, and cost nothing. These healthy experiences occur in many of the key life areas and are available within the higher level of consciousness represented by Egospiritualism.

When we refer to good, intelligent, and well-meaning people, we are referring to everyone, even those who have drifted into the worst version of themselves and have caused great pain to themselves and others. You or someone you know may be one of them. You also know a better version of yourself or that other person exists, because you have seen glimpses of that healthier person. These glimpses are reflections of the "Godness" within your being and everyone's. Unfortunately, you and others don't know how to go about becoming that person, the best version of yourself, on a full-time basis. That is why we wrote this book and our previous ones, *The Ego Unmasked: Meeting the Greatest Challenge of Your Life* (Dorrance Publishing, 2010) and *Ego and Spirituality: The Consciousness of Egospiritualism* (Balboa Press, 2012). You need to hear the voices of Ego and Spirit to become that person all of the time.

Do I need to hear both voices?

Absolutely! Transcending into higher levels of spiritual consciousness requires the transformation of the egoic voice and the energy within it. This transformation cannot occur if one fails to hear the voice of Ego and bring their egoic energy into balance where needed, regarding its power, flexibility, or vulnerability. Our interpretation of traditional messages by spiritual mentors is that they are suggesting the voice of Ego must be silenced completely in order to hear the voice of Spirit. We do not believe that is possible, because it would require the destruction of energy — human, egoic energy. This impossibility is reflected in the distance we are from world peace and the destructive insanity existent throughout the world. This insanity persists even though we are inherently good, intelligent, and well-meaning people with God in our being. An insanity which persists despite spiritual teachings and messages which have been available to us for thousands of years.

Our strategy also involves hearing and softening the voice of our ego by bringing its power, flexibility, and vulnerability into balance with the use of "mental medicine," which is thoroughly discussed in Chapters 6 to 11 of *The Ego Unmasked*. Mental medicine involves the development of relevant ego awareness and the use of reality-based thinking. This strategy transforms our ego from being our "enemy" into being our friend, in a partnership that allows us to hear the voice of Spirit and opens the door to Egospiritualism. Within this consciousness, our healthy ego self has the ability to merge and unite with our Divine Self. This partnership allows us to hear and speak with our voice — a voice in concert with the One Voice of the universe.

What will happen when I begin to hear the voices of Ego and Spirit?

Your ability to hear each of these voices will begin a shift within your consciousness on both a human and spiritual level. You will come to know the egoic energy you are living and the Divine energy that has always been available to you. This knowledge will continue to grow as you move further into ego consciousness. As you grow in your ability to recognize your egoic voice, you will become able to transform your ego into your friend and experience the best of what this energy has to offer you. You will stop surviving and start living. As you transform the voice of your ego, you'll begin to hear more of what Spirit has been saying, which you have been unable to hear.

You'll be able to hear Spirit telling you "who" God Is while showing you the Four Great Gifts that you and everyone have received. You will also come to know the various illusions your ego has been fashioning in the name of your survival, which have only served to disconnect you from God and distanced you from knowing who You truly are.

The growth in your ability to hear Ego and Spirit sets the stage for the merging of these energies and entry into the consciousness of Egospiritualism. Within this consciousness, you will come to know and live the complete awareness of who You are, who God is, and the Four Great Gifts you have received. It is within the consciousness of Egospiritualism, that you will be living at peace with yourself, the people in your life, and the world. You will be completely motivated by love in dealing with life rather than being consumed by various degrees of fear, anger, anxiety, or guilt in your efforts to manage life. You will fully respect your body, mind, and spirit rather than engaging in abuse or misuse. You will work to fulfill your life's purpose while taking advantage of all of your potential. Furthermore, you will realize that you already have everything you need and will not be consumed by artificial needs and wants, and you will be able to recognize and enjoy the things that truly matter in your life. You will be free of inappropriate or unhealthy expectations for yourself, including those that may have been placed upon you by others. You will experience a morality guided by healthiness, motivated by love rather than fear or guilt, and rooted in your truth, and you will know you don't have to be anyone else but you, anywhere else but here, and anytime else but now. You have begun to enter the Kingdom of Heaven. All of this knowledge and experience is available to you and will come as you hear the voices of Ego and Spirit.

Do I have a voice?

You can and should have a voice. However, if your ego is imbalanced, your ego is doing the talking most of the time and you are doing the listening, even though you don't realize it. Egoic energy with too much or too little power, flexibility, or vulnerability is shaping your thoughts, behaviors, feelings, and bodily experiences, for the worse. This happens in different ways for different people. Some of us become a victim, dependent, or depressive. Others become a dictator, authoritarian, racist, or perfectionist. An imbalanced ego can speak to us in many ways, and we each listen to the voice of our ego in distinctive ways. This is also how we allow ego to speak for us in our lives. Remember, this is ego's voice speaking, not our own.

This leads to the related question, *How do I replace ego's voice with my own?* You do this by learning more about what ego is, why ego is, and listening to your own distinctive egoic voice shaped by the power, flexibility, and vulnerability of your egoic energy. You can hear this voice within your thoughts, words, behaviors, feelings, and body, reflected within the "mirrors" of the key life areas, as mentioned previously. Look for patterns that occur over time; otherwise the egoic voice will do a good job of hiding from you, though this is not by intention. Upon the discovery of your egoic voice, you can begin the process of transforming it with reality-based thinking and the power of truth — a power that has been hidden from you by your imbalanced ego, which has led you into the realm of beliefs that are often well-intended but in reality misguided. This power emerges as you meet the truth that comes from living an ego that is in balance. This transformative process will be complemented by the voice of Spirit, which brings forth Divine Truths that have always resided in you and everyone. Ultimately, your voice should be spoken by you — not Ego exclusively, not Spirit exclusively, but You!

What do you mean by power, flexibility, and vulnerability issues?

Our egoic energy is comprised of power, flexibility, and vulnerability. When each of these is in balance the egoic energy leads us towards healthy reality-based thoughts, feelings, behaviors, and physiology which are used to manage our daily lives. When our egoic energy becomes imbalanced in one or more of these components we become less healthy and often get caught up in progressively non-reality-based approaches to dealing with our life, even though we are all fundamentally good, intelligent, and well-meaning persons. This difficulty is reflected in many of the key life areas we have referred to. The various roles we will be presenting in Chapters 1—6 are specific reflections of this difficulty.

Ego power issues are reflected in the ways in which people express their ideas, choices, and behaviors within the ten key life areas. Some people with higher ego power like to dominate, manipulate, or exploit others. These tendencies are often seen in roles people assume such as narcissist, dictator, exploiter, ultra-competitor, or control freak. Some people with lower ego power tend to be passive, dependent, or submissive and live in roles such as victim, dependent, depressive, under-achiever, or masochist.

Ego flexibility issues are reflected within difficulties a person has in adding, modifying, and removing knowledge within their mind. By knowledge, we mean ideas, beliefs, values, attitudes, prejudices, and illusions. Those with lower ego flexibility are often rigid, close-minded, and inflexible within their thoughts. They almost exclusively rely on the use of their own thinking and people who think very much like them. Often they believe they "own" the truth and must get others to know it. They are often seen in roles people assume such as the authoritarian, racist, religious extremist, sexist, or ethnocentrist. Those with higher ego flexibility are gullible and naïve, and they lean too much on the thinking of others. They often seek to find the truth in others, believing it could not exist within themselves. Roles they often assume include the child, cultist, loyalist, or puppet.

Finally, ego vulnerability issues are reflected in the difficulties people have in accepting their weakness and human imperfection. These issues are manifested in the susceptibility, intensity, and duration of one's fight-or-flight response and the degree of anger or fear one experiences in response to real or imagined stressors. Those with higher ego vulnerability readily experience frequent and more intensive anxiety or anger. Roles they often take on include the perfectionist, the overachiever, the traumatized, the high-maintenance partner, and the stressed-out person. Those with lower ego vulnerability often have difficulty experiencing a healthy sense of human vulnerability. In particular, they often have difficulty experiencing emotions which can be used to teach us about our weakness and imperfection. Roles they often take on include the sociopath, the loner, the logician, the hedonist, the inattentive, and the sadist.

The best answer we can give you about the meaning of power, flexibility, and vulnerability is found within the voices of Ego and Spirit. We will present numerous examples of these issues within this book. These examples, more than any definition, bring to life what we are attempting to bring to your awareness about your consciousness, ego, ego components, egoic energy, and their impact upon your human and Divine life.

What do you mean by spiritual unconsciousness?

We are specifically referring to our difficulty in knowing "who" God Is and fully recognizing the Four Great Gifts we have all been given. The former involves knowing that God Is Love, Life, Energy, and You. The latter involves recognizing the Gifts of Life, Creating Life, Eternal Life, and God Within. Many of us have heard, within religious teachings or spiritual writings, that God is present within love, life, and energy. We embrace this description because it captures what was here and everywhere before humans and human consciousness came into being. There was love embodied within the positive and transformative energy that has led to, is leading to, and will always lead to adaptation and evolution. There was life, and there has always been life to beget life. Life does not spring forth from non-life. There was energy, as energy cannot be created or destroyed. It always was, is, and will be. Each of these notions captures the essence of God.

Unfortunately, the awareness that God Is Love, Life, Energy, and You remains at a distance if one does not understand the specifics within this awareness. These specifics include the unlimited, unconditional, and connective nature of God's Love; God's presence at all times, in all places, and within all beings; and the transformative light and truth embodied within the Energy that God Is. We must also live this awareness rather than simply know it, as living versus knowing this awareness is the difference between spiritual consciousness and unconsciousness. Many good, intelligent, and well-meaning people cannot recognize this difference due to the workings and voice of their imbalanced egoic energy. An imbalanced ego often contributes to illusions such as separation, unworthiness, inequality, sensing all energy, and many more that distance us from truly knowing and living God within our life. These illusions serve to disconnect us from God and others while keeping us spiritually asleep even though we may think we have awakened.

The same goes for the Four Great Gifts. If one is only intellectually aware of them and unable to live the specifics of these Gifts, this person remains spiritually unconscious. People cannot live fully without understanding the opportunity, meaning, and purpose of their life, their ability to create life with their mind and body, their eternal life, and the presence of God within, an understanding imparted to us within the Four Great Gifts. When we are spiritually conscious, we realize we already have everything we need. Only our unconscious, imbalanced ego will tell us differently.

Is a higher level of consciousness available to everyone?

The answer is an emphatic "Yes!" This certainly may seem overly optimistic, unrealistic, and naïve, given what we said about the planet being asleep egoically and spiritually. A planet which has always been in these states of unconsciousness. A planet which has been unable to fully awaken despite the brilliant words of spiritual mentors such as Buddha, Jesus, and Muhammad, who sought to arouse us and raise our level of consciousness. Our answer also doesn't seem to square with the thoughts of other renowned writers on the topic of spiritual consciousness, which tend to suggest that living within a higher spiritual consciousness is an extreme rarity, perhaps one in ten million or greater.

Our view is an emphatic "yes" because you need not go anywhere, read anything, or meet anyone to experience higher spiritual consciousness. God's brilliance is greater than faulty requirements that humans often place upon themselves. The lived awareness that God Is Love, Life, Energy, and You can be found here, now, and within. The Great Gifts are already in your possession. You need only open your mind to live in the awareness of them. You have been empowered to take ownership of your mind and speak your voice with the free will that is within your being.

Our emphatic "yes" is also rooted in the belief this isn't a world or life meant for some and not others, or for the very few. God's brilliance is greater than human limitations, be they egoic or intellectual, that prevent us from realizing higher levels of spiritual consciousness in this lifetime or future ones, if that becomes necessary. We agree with spiritual writers who assert that higher spiritual consciousness is a rarity, if they are linking this to the elimination of one's ego. In fact, we consider eliminating one's ego impossible because it would entail the destruction of energy— human energy. Imbedded within our answer is the belief that we can be empowered with knowledge to know our ego and transform it. We can hear its voice and we can teach it what it must come to know about the suffering we have been living in the faulty name of survival. This is work we must do in concert with Spirit; it will not be done by Spirit alone.

Finally, our emphatic "yes" stems from the reality that the truth is brilliantly simple. In writing this book, we endeavored to make the consciousness discussion concrete and intellectually accessible to people while shining light directly on the two energies at the center of the discussion—Ego and Spirit. Writing in the realm of spiritual consciousness often involves unfamiliar, abstract, complex, and mystical ideas that are overwhelming to the reader. This can lead one to feel lost, defeated, and resigned to being unable to experience a higher level of spiritual consciousness and awareness, even for those who are quite intelligent or well-educated. If you have felt that way, you are not alone. We remember being in that group. In fact, most of the people who heard or read the words of the greatest consciousness teachers were unable to fully appreciate or understand them, despite these teachers' brilliance and eloquence and their frequent use of parables and stories. Many of those who have followed them intuitively sensed the truth within their words, even without a complete intellectual understanding of them. This is a reflection of the voice of Spirit within their and our being. This intuitive grasp of the truth continues in today's world. But we must do more to bring the truth onto an intellectually palatable plane in order to know the greater peace that is available to us as individuals and as a world community.

This book attempts to make the truth more accessible so that your journey can be more fruitful. *Two Voices: Ego and Spirit* will walk you along the path of consciousness while sharing with you what each voice is telling you along the journey. These voices speak directly to the thoughts, behaviors, and feelings that you are living, many of which lie at the center of the suffering and survival emphasis that dominates our lives. Again, we give an emphatic "yes" to the question of whether you can move forward into higher spiritual consciousness rooted in your ability to transform your ego, hear the voice of Spirit, and know the brilliance of truth.

We give thanks to all of the writers, teachers, actors, musicians, athletes, painters, clerics, scientists, leaders, comedians, and others who within their life's work have helped all of us to hear the voices of Ego and Spirit and the Truth within our soul.

PROLOGUE

The focus for *Two Voices: Ego and Spirit* involves not only the imbalance that can exist within our ego, but also the imbalance that often exists between our Ego and our Spirit—an imbalance between our humanity and our Divinity. This imbalance often tilts in the direction of our Ego and humanity due to our preoccupation with suffering and survival. Within this book, we will be listening to both voices' words pertaining to each of these imbalances. Before doing so, we want to introduce these voices to you. We also want to explain more about the suffering and survival that is linked to imbalance within our egoic energy, as well as the imbalance that exists between hearing the voices of Ego and Spirit.

Ego's Voice

I am going to introduce myself to you today. I will be telling you "who" I am and "why" I am in your life. This will provide you with an opportunity to know yourself better than you ever have before. You will not be hearing about me from some expert, a person who has looked from the outside at me. I will be taking you inside so you can see me from within. You will be going to the source of your humanity. The view may not always be pleasant, but it is necessary for both of us.

I will begin by telling you that I am unaware of myself or any of the ways in which I am impacting your life. I do not have a consciousness of myself, but you can develop one of me. I have no clue about the thoughts, feelings, behaviors, or physiology you are experiencing as a result of my energy. This differs from what some experts are suggesting, speaking of ego as if it were a conscious entity of itself, reflecting their ignorance of me. I cannot and do not impact you in any voluntary way. I profoundly impact you, but without volition. To intentionally impact a person requires an intellect, which is something I do not have. But you do, and you can get to know me, even though I can never know you or myself.

Before going on, I want to ask you not to flatter yourself with the notion that you already know who I am. This notion is connected to the limited view that I am mainly responsible for the amount of power or influence you need to exert in your life. That is like looking at me with a microscope possessing very low amplification. There is some truth to your notion of power. However, I am a more complex entity than that. My energy, your energy, is much more diverse, and I will be sharing that with you. Please do not feel insulted. That is not my intention, if I were able to form one. The most brilliant of minds, greatest of truth-seekers, most eloquent of philosophers, and most notable of spiritual mentors have only been able to touch upon my essence. Often they have only been able to do so in peripheral, abstract, and general ways, allowing me to remain hidden from you despite my constant presence within you and your life.

If people truly knew me, or what to do with me, there would be a lot less suffering in people's lives and the world. There would be a lot less concern about survival in the smallest and largest of matters; a lot less destruction to nature and the environment. With all of your intelligence and knowledge, would the supposedly most civilized of your countries be on the precipice of a nuclear holocaust? Would you really need to spend billions upon billions of dollars to protect people from each other—from cyber and biological terrorism—as you enter a new age? I am the true weapon of mass destruction, both personally and globally. I am the foundation and source upon which all of the others are built. This destruction is rooted in the individual and collective need for your survival. I have been exerting this impact on you throughout history and will continue to, until you get to know me and are able to transform my energy, your energy.

I remain hidden due to your ignorance and lack of awareness of me. The darkness in which I am kept allows and empowers me to impact you and everyone. I am not trying to hide from you, as I am without intention. I am just hidden due to your ignorance of me. Some have described me as only evil or as your enemy, due to their ignorance of me. I can be that, or even your devil, but I do not seek to be. Who am I, then, and what is my purpose? As I said, I am energy, a human energy. I work through the workshop of your mind, that place where ideas, beliefs, illusions, attitudes, prejudices, and knowledge are formed. I am not your mind, though many have referred to me as that. This just provides another example of their ignorance of me. I work within your mind as you draw upon my energy to shape your behaviors and feelings, and I even impact your body. I also foster the formation of your sense of self—your ego self, if you will. This is the "you" that you are or think you are, a culmination of all those things that I have impacted within the workshop of your mind. Your self is the manifestation of my energy, your energy.

You cannot change or remove any or all of your suffering from working on your self alone, or by trying to change your mind alone. They are just places to begin to find me, places to get clues and cues. You can't reach me from there. You must get to know me! And you must teach me, so I can stop teaching you. If you don't, things will really never change—for you or for humanity. Not within the darkness of your ignorance of me. You will continue to reside in the darkness of your forbearers from thousands of years ago. Things haven't changed very much, only the ways in which you try to survive and protect yourself from each other have shifted. You must get to know me so you can remove your darkness.

Some may ask, "Where did I come from and why did I come into being?" When you—meaning your very distant ancestors—left the literal or figurative Garden of Eden, in what some refer to as the Fall, I came into being. I came into being to help you survive, not only in the physical sense, but in every sense in which you exist. This effort to survive manifests within many aspects of your life, and you reflect it in your thoughts, words, and deeds. My purpose is your survival, and I protect you from anything and everything that threatens you. I protect you from people, be they friends, family, or strangers. I protect you from places, events, and experiences. When I am really getting out of balance, I am protecting you from yourself and life. This protection can be manifested in the thoughts you have, the words you use, the actions you take, the emotions you feel, and your bodily reactions. The more I am protecting you in these ways, the more you are out of balance.

You may be asking, "What do you mean by being out of balance?" As I said earlier, I am energy, an energy bounded by power, flexibility, and vulnerability. The power within this energy impacts the amount of *influence or force you exert in the name of your survival. You live this force in your words, ideas, actions, and emotions. Some of you have a great deal of this power, while many others have very little. You will be hearing more about each of these. The flexibility of your energy impacts how flexible you are in your approach to seeking truth and securing your survival. This includes how open and varied the actions and ideas are that you will use in the "challenges" to your survival that come from everyday life. Some of you are rigid and locked into only the actions and ideas that you have known thus far, while some of you are open to anything and everything that is available to you. You will be hearing more about each of these. The vulnerability of your energy impacts how intensely you experience your imperfection and need to survive. You can know this vulnerability most readily by the amount of fear or anger that you are feeling. This fear and anger can also be seen in your words, actions, and body. Some of you are consumed with your imperfection and survival, while others are oblivious to them. You will be hearing more about each of these. It is the power, flexibility, and vulnerability within your energy that shapes the thoughts, feelings, behaviors, and physiology you are using to ensure your survival.*

Some may ask, "How did I become this energy within your life?" I did not bring you to this energy. What has transpired within your life has done so. The energy I am and you are was "chosen" by life in the form of any number of unpredictable biological, social, or environmental influences that have brought your daily and mortal survival into question. Brought forth from all manner of relationships, events, injuries, circumstances, and disease which have worn upon you. You aren't responsible for their appearance at your life's door. In this sense, you are ultimately innocent and your life is quite fragile. This speaks to my intense efforts to protect you and ensure your survival.

You may ask, "Why am I telling you all this?" If I had an intention and intellect, I would tell you that I do not seek to be your enemy as others have told you. Even though I have been destructive in the name of your survival, and have caused you great suffering as others have told you, I can be your friend. It is time for your ignorance of me to end. I can be your friend, but I don't know how to do that. I do know that you cannot destroy me. You cannot dissolve, disown, or defeat me because I am energy, and you don't need to. I have love within the essence of my energy and I need you to transform it—my energy, your energy—to be your friend.

Spirit's Voice

My voice is soft and steady. It does not need to rise or fall. It speaks many things that you can only hear when you come from a place of peace and stillness to hear it. I am here and always ready to speak to you and share with you what you must come to know. You are the one who determines when that time will be and whether it will come in this earthly life, the next, or beyond. It is your choice to enter the Kingdom of Heaven, not mine. When you hear my voice, these are the things you will come to know and live.

I Am—the Love within your being. The source of Love that is unconditional, unlimited, and connective within all beings, when you truly know who I am.

I Am—the Life within your being. The source of Life that is present, honored, and respected within all beings, when you truly know who I am.

I Am—the Energy within your being. The source of light and truth that is transformative within all beings, when you truly know who I am.

I Am—the Gift of Life, so that you will know meaning and purpose within all of the abundance available to you within the Kingdom of Heaven.

I Am—the Gift of Creating Life, so you will do great works with your mind and body to enter the Kingdom of Heaven.

I Am—the Gift of Eternal Life, so you are always welcome within the time and place of your choosing to enter the Kingdom of Heaven.

I Am—the Gift of God Within, so you can be guided to all that is within you, the Kingdom of Heaven.

Ego brings about the construction of many illusions, which foster distance between who You are and who I Am.

Ego has led to your believing that you are separate from others and God. Any separation is an illusion of your own making brought forth from your ego. God can be nowhere else but within you, at all times and within all places, as with all living beings. Through God, you are connected to all things as One. This you must come to know. This you must teach your ego.

Ego has led to your believing that questions of worthiness exist within yourself and others of God. An illusion which has often led you to believe that you and others are unworthy of God, and that God therefore cannot be in your presence. This illusion has also led you to know yourself as unworthy of others or they of you. There can be no unworthiness as all persons are the expression of God in human form. This you must come to know. This you must teach your ego.

Ego has led to your believing that life forms are unequal and deserve different levels of respect. This illusion is often applied within the human species as well as across different life forms—a source for abusive treatment of others in the faulty name of survival. There can be no inequality or different levels of respect for any life form because God is existent within all species. This you must come to know. This you must teach your ego.

Ego has led to your believing that God can only be known through the power of your physical senses and human mind. An illusion failing to recognize the broader reality and greater Truth existent within the Divine Realm which cannot be fully known within human senses and beliefs, alone. This illusion brings boundaries and limitations to your understanding of God. These weaken your awareness of God's constant presence, availability, and influence within your life and all of life. The unseen will be seen and the unknown will be known upon entering the Divine Realm. This you must come to know. This you must teach your ego.

Ego has led to your believing that you are not safe when matters are beyond your human control. A belief rooted in the illusion that ultimate control and order resides within the earthly realm. A control framed by human expectations, attachments, and guarantees you have constructed to ensure your survival. An illusion often blinding you to the difference between faulty wants and genuine needs. This illusion prevents you from knowing that you already have everything you need within the Divine Gifts. This illusion also fails to recognize the existence of Divine Order. An Order resting upon Divine Truth. When one is being the Love, Life, and Energy God Is all will be as it should be. This you must come to know. This you must teach your ego.

Ego has led to your fashioning a completely human understanding of disorder and chaos built only upon earthly beliefs. This illusion fails to recognize that difficult, painful, or unpleasant challenges going on in your life or in the world are often a call to know human and Divine Truth. Suffering and earthly disorder is brought about when living beneath human and Divine Truth. Let Divine Order embrace earthly disorder within Divine Truth. An Order in which you are being the Love, Life, and Energy God Is within your earthly work. This you must come to know. This you must teach your ego.

Ego does not know me at all. It cannot hear my voice. It can only come to know my voice through you. However, it can weaken your ability to hear my voice. The greater your egoic energy, the weaker is your ability to hear my voice. You replace it with a voice shaped by ego with beliefs rather than truth, which distorts, disturbs, and destroys your efforts to hear my voice and to know God. When you are able to soften the voice of ego with your own voice born of truth, earthly and Divine, you will begin to hear more of my voice, as I am always here to be heard, as I am a part of you.

Ego's ignorance of who God Is, the Divine Gifts you have been given, and the illusions it is perpetrating are the basis for your suffering. I will be sharing more of what ego does not know about me after it has told you more about its work. For now, I will leave this moment by telling you that ego is the lost part of your soul, which does not know how to heal itself, and which doesn't know that it doesn't have to ensure your survival. It has you believing that you must survive by living from your ego. Together, we can help ego to be healed, learn that it does not have to help you to survive in ways that bring suffering, and allow you to make your way home along the path you must take to the Kingdom of Heaven.

Suffering and Survival

You have and will continue to hear a great deal about suffering and survival from the voices of Ego and Spirit. Suffering and survival serve as major obstacles to our movement along the consciousness path and into higher levels of spiritual consciousness. Unless we come to know the ways in which we are suffering and why it is happening, we will continue to repeat this suffering and remain unable to fully know the greatness available within our humanity and Divinity. We will remain stuck in our suffering by an ego preoccupied with our survival. A survival not only in the mortal sense, but also in the daily sense. A preoccupation with daily survival in the key life areas often brings us into unrecognized suffering. Suffering and survival as we often experience a sense of battling with people, loved ones, work, achievement, change, adversity, stressors, and our emotions.

Often, we can only fully know our suffering in retrospect and not as we are living within it. Only upon awakening to ourselves, God, and the Great Gifts do we recognize the suffering we were living in the name of survival and how much we have missed. A person who has awakened from egoic unconsciousness often thinks, "I didn't know who I was being and all of the damage I was doing to myself and others." It is our hope that from our work people will awaken sooner rather than later so they can do more living and less suffering within this lifetime.

You may be thinking, "Really? Is that all there is to it—just stop trying to survive, and all of my suffering will end?" or "That's too simplistic; it has got to be more complicated than that!" Well, yes and no. Yes, it is more complicated than that when you get into a more precise and in-depth understanding of what is meant by suffering and survival, a depth we believe parallels Buddha's pronouncement that "all is suffering." No, when you hear the voice of Spirit teaching you about who You are, who God Is, and the Four Great Gifts you have been given—and when you come to know the power of living within truth, both human and Divine. This is when you can teach ego with your voice to relinquish its need to help you survive in unnecessary ways, and your suffering begins to drift away.

This often happens to people who have come to terms with a terminal illness and their human mortality. If you listen to the grace within their words and actions, you can see how they have stopped being consumed with their survival. They are embracing each day, each moment, and each experience with a depth they had not fully known. They will often tell you they aren't dying, but have started living. They have relinquished the ego-driven need to survive in the human sense and embraced the eternal life coming from the voice of Spirit. Truth is replacing belief, and there is no longer any fear. This is a rather dramatic, though real, example of what we are referring to when we talk about freeing ourselves from ego's struggle for our survival. Fortunately, we can relinquish the ego-based need for survival and the suffering it causes us without facing the difficult and challenging life circumstances of the terminally ill person. We can live with the same grace and depth as such a person may be living when we have awakened egoically and spiritually.

Before proceeding, we would like to make an important distinction between healthy and unhealthy ways that people deal with suffering. The former include choices that we make to optimize the opportunities available to us within this current existence. They include appropriate efforts to meet physical, mental, or emotional needs through options such as diet, exercise, rest, entertainment, prayer, meditation, yoga, and medication. These are all healthy options that a balanced ego can bring us to in order to embrace and enjoy this life. These strategies do not involve suffering. We also make appropriate choices to ensure our survival when others jeopardize our physical safety or survival. There is nothing wrong with healthfully protecting ourselves and others in ways that allow us to experience what has been made available to us in this lifetime.

The latter involve unhealthy choices driven by egoic issues involving power, flexibility, or vulnerability that lead us into unneeded suffering occurring in the name of our daily physical, mental, or emotional survival. These include exaggerations, distortions, beliefs, and even lies we tell ourselves or others that lead to suffering. We can experience this suffering in our thoughts, words, behaviors, feelings, and physical well-being. Imbalanced egoic energy can bring us to these forms of suffering rather easily and very often, even though we don't know it. We will be providing you with many specific examples of how this suffering may be manifesting in your life, or in the lives of people you know or live with, as we listen more to the voices of Ego and Spirit and learn about them.

Suffering and survival are intimately linked. The more consumed you are, or your ego is, with your survival, the more you are suffering. You may be asking the perfectly normal question, "If I were suffering, wouldn't I know it?" Often embedded within this question is the notion that if you were suffering, you would be experiencing pain. On the physical level, we often do experience suffering in the form of pain in the aftermath of an injury, illness, or disease. This suffering can persist to varying degrees until the original source of the pain has been healed or resolved. When people apply this frame of reference to the mental, emotional, or spiritual realm, they can easily conclude that no suffering is transpiring because they are not experiencing any physical pain. This is often an erroneous conclusion because the suffering taking place in one's thoughts, words, deeds, or feelings can be much more subtle. The perfectionist, the racist, the narcissist, the sociopath, and many more people who you will be hearing about from the voices of Ego and Spirit are all suffering, but they often don't realize it. They are experiencing more pain within their thoughts, words, deeds, or feelings than they can recognize. For them, the absence of suffering is actually an illusion.

You may be asking, "If I am suffering and don't know it, what's wrong with that?" or "Aren't you giving me a problem that I don't know I have?" The answer to these questions is that you are living a lesser version of yourself and life than is possible. You are getting less rather than more. Your response may be, "Isn't it all relative?" or "If I don't know what I am missing in life, I won't miss it," or "What I don't know won't hurt me." This collection of responses can all be filed under the "ignorance is bliss" approach to life. There is one major problem with this approach, you already know that you are suffering. The voice of Spirit is a part of you and is speaking your truth to you even though you may not hear it. It is letting you know that you are at a distance from the best version of yourself. That may seem like bad news to you, but ultimately it is very good news. It means that you and everyone else is here to transform and transcend their humanity, to live and experience all that is available within God's Kingdom. No one can be left out or left behind. There can be no other way than the path home to God. It may take several lifetimes, but that is your destiny.

The final question we will speak to before listening to the voices of Ego and Spirit is, "If I am really not suffering or trying to survive, how would I know it?" If this holds true for you, you will know it because you are living in peace with yourself, the people in your life, and the world; you are completely motivated by love rather than fear, anger, anxiety, or guilt in your efforts to deal with life; you fully respect your body, mind, and spirit rather than engaging in abuse or misuse of them; you are working to fulfill your life's purpose with the full use of your potential; you realize you have everything you need and are not consumed by artificial wants and needs; you recognize and enjoy the things that truly matter; you are free of inappropriate or unhealthy expectations of yourself or those placed upon you by others; you experience a morality guided by healthiness, motivated by love rather than fear or guilt, and rooted in your truth; and you know you don't have to be anyone else but you, anywhere else but here, and anytime else but now. Anything less than this is suffering. When you reside in this realm of egospiritualistic consciousness, you will have no unnecessary concern with survival and will have no need to suffer.

THE AWAKENING

Two Voices

The ego unconsciousness from which one must awaken is a consciousness in which little if any awareness of one's ego and its impact upon one's life exists. Your ego's power, flexibility, and vulnerability is impacting many important areas of your life, such as work, relationships, achievement, adversity, change, stress, and conflict. These are the places in which your ego is often speaking, but you don't know it. It is speaking to you within the words, thoughts, feelings, behaviors, and bodily experiences that fill up your life. The greater the difficulty you are experiencing, the more your ego is speaking for you, and the more egoically unconscious you are.

Ego unconsciousness is also quite diverse, with its impact depending on the degree to which our egoic energy is imbalanced in its power, flexibility, and vulnerability. We can be egoically unconscious, but in different ways from others. Consequently, finding our way out of this darkness means we must "walk" along our own distinct path that we have made for ourselves. A path defined by awakening to the voice of our ego and learning what it has led us to in the name of our survival. It is a path built upon reality-based thinking and human truth as well as Divine Truth.

Our egoic awakening will also allow us to fully awaken to the voice of our Spirit.

Despite being a dark, unrecognized, or unknown place, ego unconsciousness isn't necessarily a "bad" place of consciousness. Many people can be living full, satisfying lives even if they are unaware of how their ego is impacting their lives. You may be one of them. These are healthy people whose egoic energy is in balance or close to balance regarding its power, flexibility, and vulnerability. They can also be experiencing a higher spiritual consciousness, even if they are egoically unconscious. The voice of ego is not causing deafness to the voice of their Spirit. Thus, ego consciousness is not a requirement for a healthy human and spiritual existence. An ego that is in balance, even if you are unaware of it, *is*. However, one caution is necessary: Your ego can have you believing that things in your human and spiritual life are better than they really are. Lots of people live within the illusion of human and spiritual health, even though those surrounding them can often see through this illusion. How would you know whether that is or isn't the case for yourself? Look at the aspects of your life we have described as being reflective of the consciousness of egospiritualism. That is where the answer lies. One cannot truly live a genuinely healthy, happy human and spiritual life in their absence. One cannot be living in this place of consciousness with an imbalanced ego. The greater the imbalance, the greater the illusion one is living of human and spiritual wellness.

For many, ego unconsciousness has always been a dark and bad place. Since very early in their lives, all they seem to have known is suffering and misery, as reflected in painful thoughts, feelings, behaviors, and bodily experiences with which they are trying to cope and survive. The emphasis on suffering and survival is often rooted in dysfunctional families and traumatic events that have confronted them with abuse, whether physical, mental, emotional, or sexual. Abuse which may have been "forgotten" as they have gotten older, but has not been resolved. A lack of resolution reflected in painful thoughts, feelings, behaviors, and bodily experiences that they are "chained" to. Ego is a very loud but unrecognized voice in their survival.

Aside from the brief glimpses they may get of a better life, many of them become resigned to a life that is far less than it could be.

For them, there is no greater life to be known. These traumatic relationships and events have caused significant imbalance in their egoic energy, with which they are trying to survive, via power, flexibility, or vulnerability issues. Many also become fixated on the available pseudo-happiness options often put forth by a commercial industry that partially exists to numb their pain or to provide a substitute for the genuine happiness they are missing and have never known. Unfortunately, these are only temporary solutions that offer symptomatic soothing or masking of deeper underlying problems based in the power, flexibility, and vulnerability issues of their ego. These problems exist within rather than without, and these are the kind of problems you will be hearing about from the voices of Ego and Spirit. Fortunately, these problems can be addressed with the development of ego awareness, transformation of one's egoic energy, and listening to the voice of Spirit.

For many, entry into unhealthy ego unconsciousness comes further up the road in their lives, within their adolescence or adulthood. Circumstances in people's lives can connect them to the wrong people, places, or situations that can transform healthy, balanced egoic energy into unhealthy, imbalanced egoic energy. Various forms of abuse, destructive relationships, and substance involvement are significant examples of this process at work—a process that has preyed upon the person's ego, which in its efforts to help a person survive has become progressively imbalanced in its power, flexibility, or vulnerability. Many people have fallen into this dark, difficult, and destructive place of suffering due to the circumstances in their lives, impacting themselves as well as loved ones. We can come to this place even if we have had the most supportive of families and upbringing, and even though this place might make no sense to ourselves or those closest to us. The senselessness of such changes reflects the often-fragile nature of human life. At the center of this senselessness resides an unhealthy, imbalanced ego struggling to help us survive in often the most destructive of ways. This ego must be transformed back into health. Everyone has the ability to undertake the transformative process, in which we work to hear the voices of Ego and Spirit that are speaking to us. The more we hear and understand them, the greater the opportunity to undertake this transformative journey.

There is one other group of egoically unconscious people who are feeling "unsettled." Things are often going reasonably well in their lives, or seem to be. Still, they have the sense that there is something more or something missing in their lives. These people are likely to be feeling pretty good about their life situation and may question their right to complain about anything when others seem to be experiencing more difficulty. They may have a good car, home, family, marriage, job, and health, yet things don't seem completely right. What's missing? Themselves, or more specifically, the best version of themselves, the person we call You. They may have done an excellent job of procuring all of the things we associate with having a "good life," except themselves. Many of us have bought into the idea that we must simply procure these things to have a good life, often instilled during our formative years. We remember that person well in our own previous life experiences.

As time goes on, the sense of being unsettled often grows, particularly as our children get older, if we have kids. They are able to get on with their lives without our immediate guidance and support. We are no longer distracted by their needs and can pay more attention to our own. The voice of Spirit may be getting louder at this time, with many of the things it is saying coming to us intuitively, if not intellectually. Spirit may be calling us to better know ourselves, who God Is, and what the Four Great Gifts we have been given are. It may be calling us to a greater life than the one we have been living, no matter how good it has been, and urging us to step beyond our humanity and further into our Divinity.

As we have said, ego unconsciousness is quite diverse as is the suffering brought forth within various forms of egoic imbalance. Within the next several chapters, Ego and Spirit will be speaking specifically about this diversity which is often reflected within the roles we and others may assume in our lives. Their words will help you to understand this breadth, an understanding that will help you to better understand others as well as yourself. Through this understanding, you will come to a greater awakening to your Ego and Spirit.

CHAPTER 1

Higher Ego Power Energy

Ego's Voice

I foster a great deal of power within your being, a power you use to experience and exercise control in all that you wish within your life. This power does not need to recognize any earthly boundaries in what you want to think, feel, or do. You can use this power to survive in every area of your life to which it may be called upon. This power allows you to resist or control all of the challenges life may bring to you—challenges coming forth within people, work, loved ones, achievement, change, adversity, stressors, and conflict that enter your life. This power also allows you to feel the pleasure and happiness you want to feel, and the will to use any means necessary to getting it.

Through your power, I am helping you to dominate, control, or know more than others. You are to believe that listening to others is not necessary; that listening to others, thinking what they think, or doing what they do would be weakness, an experience that is foreign to you. Others cannot really know more than you do. Your way is right and doesn't need to be challenged or changed; theirs does. Changing yourself would be foolishness, and a sign of weakness. You can mistreat people when necessary, know that you are better than them, underestimate them where needed; insist on doing things the best or right way, which is your way; and to be overly confident.

You must stay independent from those who are closest to you, be they your spouse or partner, children, siblings, or parents. They cannot know as much as you do or influence you. That would be weakness. You must fail

5

to communicate, compromise, or show compassion, since that would signal weakness to them. You need to do most of the thinking in the relationships with the people who are closest to you, so everyone can be protected by your wisdom. I help you to insist on your partner becoming as much like you as possible, in his or her approach to things, so your partner can be a better person—you.

You are to love yourself more than anyone else, someone others can love even more than they love themselves, and someone who is more important than everyone else. Recognize that all criticism of you is destructive, only intended to weaken you. You must know that you are entitled to and deserve all of the love that others can give to you, love that you can use to further empower yourself.

It is with your power that you can achieve all that you want or can, so that you can shine and show others that you are better than they are. This way, you won't have to experience the weakness of others, who are below you. You must know them as enemies seeking to take the victory that only belongs to you. You are to win or achieve at all costs, so that you will not need to taste defeat, or experience it for very long if it occurs. Minimize or underestimate what others have achieved in order to keep you above them. Your achievements represent the power and control you have over others as well as yourself.

Resist very strongly what others would have you think or believe. Changing your mind due to the influence of others would represent weakness, a loss of power, and control, an experience I have made foreign and forbidden to you. You are to think that you already know everything you need to know, and that it is the thinking of others that must change. Changing the thinking of others allows you to experience even more power.

You must control all of the change that comes into your life. Changes must meet with your approval, lest you see them as demonstrating your weakness. Impose boundaries upon change involving your health, relationships, finances, work, or family members. Any of the changes occurring in these aspects of your life must meet with your approval. If not, resist, undo, or avoid them, changing the change, so you are the one who has the control. You must know that the only good changes are the ones you instigate, not others or life.

Know that all of the adversity and problems life brings you are an attempt to lessen your power and weaken you. Failures, losses, or mistakes that occur are not truly of your making, but stem from the weakness of *others or the imperfect nature of life. You do not need to own responsibility for their occurrence. These are things that others must take care of, with your guidance, if necessary. Failure is not an option, as it would represent weakness and a lack of power—an experience I have helped you to see as foreign and forbidden to you.*

Your power is the source of obtaining all of the things that can provide you with pleasure and happiness in your life—money, status, power, people, objects, places, and experiences. They are the means to your happiness that exists within your control. Anything and everything that you desire for pleasure and happiness must and will become yours. I also help you to show these acquisitions to others as reflections of your power, control, and happiness to which there are no limits. You are the master of your domain; you are surviving well.

You must conquer all of the stressors that life brings to you, whether they involve loved ones, health, work, finances, or relationships. Make them go away, or to go your way. These stressors challenge your power, and these problems must be vanquished as you see fit. This can include believing that you are more powerful than the stressors, immune to the stressors, not experiencing stress when you are, or minimizing the stressors. Know that asking for help in the management of stressors is an act of weakness.

You are to believe that winning in a conflict represents power and control, while losing represents weakness and the absence of control. You must win in all conflicts, be they about large or small matters. The issue is secondary to the power and control at stake. You must win to establish or maintain your power, your control. Losing would be like dying. You need not be concerned about the losers, because losing is the price they must pay for challenging your power and control. They are only getting what they deserve, the pain of defeat. There can only be one victor, and you must be that person.

Spirit's Voice

You exist within a tremendous amount of suffering. A suffering born from the profound ignorance of not knowing who You are, who God Is, and the Divine Gifts you have been given. The ignorance of yourself has been met with the need for a great deal of power to replace that which you don't know, a power that you fully embrace to ensure your daily survival. This power, however, is only helping you to exist rather than live and slowly die in the earthly sense. In the process, it is distorting and removing a part of your soul that allows you to know your Divine Truth and the Love, Life, and Energy God Is.

Your earthly power is keeping you at great distance from God even though God exists within you. You prefer this distance because God can only be a rival to your power and control. Hearing my voice would only ruin things for you, because you want to be your own god, and when possible, god for others. You may seek God in times of desperation, but only as a tool to maintain your power and control. Upon awakening you will learn that much greater power has been made available to you.

Your suffering manifests from the various illusions you have constructed and are employing within many areas of your life in the service of your earthly power. While you do not recognize this daily suffering, it can be revealed to you as you awaken to my voice. This will be a painful but necessary awakening that can move you beyond your suffering and into the joy and happiness for which you are destined.

The illusions of unworthiness and inequality you see within others have been fashioned to grow the sense of empowerment you hold amongst others. This is an empowerment in which you can only feel safe when being greater than others. You know others as only being separate from and unequal to you so they cannot challenge you and lessen your power. This separation and inequality can only be maintained within your struggle to accumulate power.

You embrace your earthly senses and mind as allowing you to know all that can be known in the service of your power and control. It is within this illusion that you know yourself as the rightful person to control others. The illusion of an absolute earthly control has led you to seek to be its source within your earthly empowerment. It is within this illusion that you seek to impose an order of your making in which you feel most safe and can survive. Each of these illusions will have no purpose and dissolve as you awaken to the power within your Divinity.

The Love God Is, is greater than any earthly power you possess. A Love which can remove darkness and bring forth light so that you can truly know your empowerment. A Love which is always available and without conditions for giving or receiving to fully empower. A Love in which illusions of unworthiness, inequality, or separation cannot exist to empower oneself or disempower others. It is within this Love that you are fully empowered beyond that which can be known in the earthly realm.

The Life God Is, is one of empowerment, not for some but for all. It is not for you to remove the empowerment of others within the illusions of separation, unworthiness, and inequality you have fashioned. You cannot own the life of others within the service of your earthly empowerment. You can only be lifeless within the ownership and control you seek within your thoughts, words, and deeds. All of them are a reflection of your suffering.

The Energy God Is, is infinite and present within all times, all places, and all beings. It cannot be contained within boundaries fashioned by your illusions. Boundaries intended to affirm the reach of your earthly power. Your awakening to this Energy will show that you and others have been empowered and are destined for greater things than can be known only within the earthly realm.

The Gift of Life is given with complete empowerment. You need not seek what has been given in Divine Truth. Your life is not to be only a tool, a time, or a opportunity to fulfill all of your earthly desires. You can only reject the awareness of this Gift and make a lifeless life within the false empowerment you seek within the earthly realm. Awaken to your true empowerment so you can fully know your meaning and purpose from this Gift within being the Love, Life, and Energy God Is.

The Gift of Creating Life empowers you to fashion thoughts, words, and deeds of service to you and your neighbor. A Gift to be known within all of your earthly gifts which are to be used while being the Love, Life, and Energy God Is. It is not a Gift to be used for harmful or destructive creations in the service of your earthly empowerment. The truly empowered have no need for such creations as they can only bring forth suffering to those whom they touch.

The Gift of Eternal Life will empower you to walk fearlessly in your earthly life. You need not resist illness, aging, or death with illusions of empowerment over them. A resistance comprised of denial and rejection leading you to work against them and not with them. It is within this resistance to your earthly weakness and mortality that you have brought suffering to yourself and others. You have been given in your Divinity what cannot be known in your humanity, eternal life. You can only transform and transcend within your earthly life as you move forward on your path to the Kingdom of Heaven.

The Gift of God Within cannot be removed within illusions of your earthly empowerment. A power which has embraced separation, unworthiness, and inequality to place you above others while removing the awareness of God's presence within you and your neighbor. Your power is not great enough to remove God from your being, only the awareness of this Gift. As you awaken to this Gift you will know your true empowerment and that all has been made possible for everyone within Divine Truth.

The Dictator

The Dictator believes that he has the right to control how others must think, feel, and behave. He knows himself as greater than others by virtue of his intellect, talent, or money. He has a sense of superiority that entitles him to exert unquestioned influence on others. He becomes extremely angered by those who may question him or who are seen as seeking to reduce his power. This often leads him to strive to remove this challenge with responses that are often abusive. He is often blind to this abuse due to the power that consumes him.

Ego's Voice

I am the source of your intense need to dominate the people who surround you in your life. You are led to believe that your way is the right way and must prevail; therefore, you have no need to listen to or communicate to others. That would only involve getting poor ideas and choices, which would weaken you. You do not need to feel compassion for the mistakes or weaknesses of others. Their pain is the cost for failing to do things the way you know they should be done. Your compassion takes the form of leading them to a better understanding of how to do things. Domination is your oxygen, the means to your safety and survival and you must have it.

You must get people to do things and think the way you do by any means possible. These people can be your children, partner, friends, employees, or acquaintances. The means by which you persuade them can include intimidation, coercion, manipulation, exploitation, or abuse. You must think of them as being weaker and incapable of leading themselves. They must be led, and you must do the leading. Your greater abilities were meant to do this leading. Anyone else's leadership or guidance must be challenged or defeated. If you or others followed them, it would represent weakness and a threat to your survival.

You are entitled to feel angry when others fail or refuse to do your will. You are also entitled to use this anger as a force to alter their will, when and where necessary. The consequences they receive are the price they must pay for violating your will—a will that knows what is good and right for everyone. You are also entitled to destroy those who would stand in your way. They intend to weaken you and threaten your survival. You must meet their force with overwhelming force to eliminate their threat to you.

People are not entitled to be angry with you and any of their anger toward you is misplaced. They fail to understand that you are only attempting to help them with your knowledge, understanding, and guidance. They should be loving you instead, as what you offer them is intended to help make them stronger rather than remaining in their weakness. You are being generous to them, as you are not only working to ensure your survival, but theirs as well.

Spirit's Voice

The excessive power within your humanity has greatly distanced you from your Divinity. It is within your power that illusions of separation, inequality, and unworthiness have been fashioned with which to know your neighbor. These illusions have also led you to know yourself as all-powerful and separated from God. The Love, Life, and Energy God Is within all beings is unknown to you. Your Divinity can be known with the awareness that God Is Love and that you have the Gift of God Within your being.

You do not know the Love that truly exists in your being. It has been replaced by thoughts, words, and deeds filled with anger and hatred that you are using to dominate others. All of these are reflections of the suffering that you do not realize you are living. Each creating greater distance from the Love God Is within your being. You are also visiting this suffering upon others in your efforts to dominate them. Domination intended to serve your need for power while making your neighbor separated, less equal, and unworthy of you. As your earthly power grows so does your suffering and the distance from God within you and within your neighbor.

You exist as if you were alone and isolated in your dealings with people. You are also unable to recognize the presence of God within others. This ignorance has made people dangerous and threatening to you, and you feel you must resist this danger and threat with your power and control. You don't really know other people at all, which is a reflection of your suffering.

You cannot truly love them or be loved by them, because you believe this would threaten your survival, another reflection of your suffering.

God's absence in your awareness has led you to the illusion of being all-powerful, superior to others, and not in need of God in your life. Great human power has led you to have no limits or boundaries in your dealings with people. Everything is at your disposal, you believe—even those thoughts, words, or deeds that are destructive and harmful to others, and ultimately, to yourself. This is a reflection of your suffering. Your inability to know the equality of all human beings, built upon your notion of supremacy, has made you callous and insensitive to them, another reflection of your suffering. Your lack of need for God has blinded you to who you truly are and led you to walk a lonely path filled with anger, hatred, and destruction, all further reflections of your suffering.

The Rebel

The Rebel has a very difficult time accepting any form of authority that may be directed toward her. Her responses often involve doing the opposite or something very different than what has been asked of her. These responses are intended to show how far removed she is from the control that others would attempt to exert upon her. Unfortunately, her rebellion often takes a very immature and dysfunctional approach, which ultimately leads her into greater difficulty.

Ego's Voice

I am the source of your intense need to reject the world and those in it, particularly those who want to be your source of authority and who may attempt to control you. You must strive to reject them all, be they parents, bosses, teachers, police officers, spouses, or coaches, as well as the rules or boundaries they may attempt to impose upon you. You must also recognize that all of their words, rules, expectations, and consequences are just ways to manipulate and control you. These forms of control are not meant to help you, but to harm you. You, and only you, are to be your authority. Allowing authority to only reside in you is helping you to hold on to your power. Rebellion is your oxygen, and you must have it. It will ensure your safety and survival.

You are to view any and all other authority as destructive, believing its only intention is to weaken and then destroy you. You must reject it in order to survive. You are not fooled by others' supposedly good intentions. They are only trying to weaken you with this disguise. They are acting in their own best interests, not yours. They cannot ensure your survival; only you can.

You must form a strong connection between rejection and empowerment. The more you reject, the stronger you feel. You can feel strongest and safest when you are rejecting and rebelling, particularly those who would seek to be your authority. You are empowered by all of the thoughts, words, and deeds you have been led you to in your rebellion. You can use them all to construct a fortress in which you have been protected and can survive. Do not venture forth from this fortress with communication, compromise, or compassion, lest you be weakened and your survival brought into question. Following rules, meeting obligations, giving in to others, and listening to others are all ways to become weaker, lessening your power. You must not do any of these things within your home, work, or community. You must keep others at a distance with the thoughts, words, and deeds you have learned to keep you safe and to ensure your survival.

Spirit's Voice

Your intense desire for power is blinding you to the Gift of God Within your being and the Love God Is that is present in all beings, including yourself. You are existing, and attempting to survive, at a great distance from this awareness. For you, there is no higher power than that which resides in your human self. You are unable to fully embrace God because this notion represents a threat to your power and authority. You view God as an authority who will only try to make you as weak as everyone else within the human realm. This is an illusion and a reflection of your suffering, as God can only empower you and can never weaken you. God's presence within your being fully empowers you. There is no need for daily suffering in the form of thoughts, words, or deeds intended to reject others and to empower you. These faulty efforts to empower you become unnecessary as you recognize the Gift of God Within your being and your true empowerment.

The blindness of your intense human power is often preventing you from knowing the Love God Is, though this Love is frequently reflected in the *work of those you are rejecting and rebelling against. You have frequently responded to this Love with the anger and fear that fuel your thoughts, words, and deeds. These emotions are reflections of your suffering, as you believe you live in a world where you must be wary and on your guard, a world that does not know the Love God Is in yourself and others, a world in which you are unable to discern those who truly seek to impact you for your greater good. These are reflections of your suffering.*

Your blindness has also destroyed your ability to exercise authority for the best interests of others. Your power has taught you to use authority to control people, rather than to love them. This control is often motivated by anger and fear and is reflected in thoughts, words, and deeds that are expressions of suffering. You, as well as all beings, are intended to help, teach, and guide others. However, the words you teach others must be energized by the Love God Is. This Love truly empowers you and allows you to know there is no need for the suffering that comes from rejection and rebellion.

The Narcissist

The Narcissist has fallen in love with himself and wants others to do so as well, even if the other person must love themself less. He has an intense air of self-importance that diminishes those who surround him. His needs are of the utmost importance and must be met before those of others can be considered. People only exist to meet his needs. He greatly confuses wants and needs, viewing them as being the same thing. Furthermore, he has great difficulty recognizing any weaknesses within himself, only noticing his strengths. He is likely to disown those persons who would seek to point out any of his weaknesses to him.

Ego's Voice

I am the source of your intense need to love yourself and to have others love you. You are to view and experience love as a means to empowerment when you receive it from yourself or others. The more love you can give to yourself or get from others, the more powerful you can feel. There are no boundaries to the means by which you can obtain this love. You are to believe that you are deserving of it all and that no one and nothing can stand in your way. Love is your oxygen, and you must have it to be safe and to survive.

Recognize love in any of the thoughts, words, or actions of others, even if it is not real. It is important for you to experience love, whether real or fictitious, so that you can feel empowered and survive. Their absence, or your failure to recognize them as love, would cause you to slowly die. This must be avoided and you must also readily notice or find the withholding of love from you by friends or family. You can see it in their thoughts, words, or deeds. They are withholding something that rightfully belongs to you. They are also trying to weaken you with their rejection of you by withholding love from you. You must meet this rejection with rejection by withholding your love from them or insist that they start giving you what you rightfully deserve.

You must hold on to your love and to not give it away. Giving away love to others in thoughts, words, and deeds is giving them power, and it serves to weaken you, which you must avoid. At the very least, they must return your love to ensure that you have not been weakened. You are to believe that love cannot be freely given. There is always a price that must be paid immediately and in full. People cannot owe you love. That would lessen your power, weaken you, and threaten your survival.

Spirit's Voice

Your intense power has blinded you to the true meaning of love and its constant presence in your life. For you, love is like a fuel or a resource that must be replenished to ensure your survival. The continual efforts you make to replenish it within your thoughts, words, and deeds are reflections of your suffering, which is seen in the faulty distortions, expectations, and conditions you have fashioned for giving and receiving love. With Love, there is no giving or receiving; there is just being.

You seek to replenish something you already have and have always had. Your failure to realize that God Is Love and that you have the Gift of God Within has led you to look elsewhere for these things. This journey, fashioned by your power, has been filled with faulty notions and misunderstandings of Love. It has included faulty infatuation with yourself, needing others to have this infatuation with you, rejection of others, and the misperception of rejection from others. These are all reflections of suffering due to your misunderstanding of Love rooted in your intense need for power.

Your intense power has also led you into illusions of unworthiness and inequality within your neighbor. Each shares the notion of your supremacy among all beings. You look upon others as less worthy of your love and less entitled to the treatment that you expect from others. Your suffering is reflected in the thoughts, words, and deeds you employ in your dealings with those beings you see as less worthy and less equal to you. This suffering can end when you awaken to the awareness that God Is Life and existent within all life. Within this awareness, there can be no "greater than" or "less than." All beings are equal, as God is present within all beings. To see oneself as greater than others is to see oneself as greater than God.

The Ultra-Competitor

The Ultra-Competitor approaches life as a series of competitions. These competitions can occur at any time or in any place, and they can involve large or small matters. A win-at-all-costs mentality often drives her. Winning is the only thing that matters to her, and failure is not an option. She perceives winning and experiencing a sense of power and control as closely linked. Winning is the main way to feed her intense needs for power and control. In the event of a "loss," she is likely to seek another competition to rectify her discomfort. Until this occurs, she is likely to beat herself up for her loss.

Ego's Voice

I am the source of your need to outperform all others. It does not matter whether the stakes are high or low; the opponent young or old, a loved one or stranger; and the task significant or menial. You must prevail and stand above all others. You cannot fail or lose, lest you be weakened. Others cannot see you as weakened or think less of you. To do so would threaten your survival. Winning is your oxygen, and you must have it to ensure your safety and survival.

You must view all competitors as enemies. There is no place for friends or friendship in the arena. They seek to take the victory that should belong only to you. They seek to weaken you by showing they are better than you.

You have learned that they seek to take your power and you can never let this happen. Losses are like slow forms of death that threaten your survival. Success and victory is what will keep you alive. The more the better and the greater is your ability to survive. Competition and competitors must be met with whatever means necessary to assure your victory. You must use whatever thoughts, words, or deeds you can attach to your opponents in order to win. Hate them if you must; demonize them if you can. Break, revise, or ignore any rules that may be necessary to assure victory. Your survival is more important than the context in which it is occurring. This end justifies the means.

There is no place for humility, only exaltation for yourself and from others in the aftermath of your victory. Humility and shame belongs to those you have vanquished. They have challenged you and lost. They must bear the consequences for what they have done in attempting to steal your victory and power. You must bask in the victory that affirms your power, and you must never know their humility or shame. To do so would threaten your survival.

Spirit's Voice

The intense power within your humanity is blinding you to the Love and Life which God Is within you and all beings. You have become loveless and lifeless within your hunger for power and success. A hunger in which you seek to place yourself above all others within your earthly life. The enemy you have come to know in the arena is not your neighbor, but yourself. Your victory and success cannot ensure your survival any more than it can remove that of your neighbor. They can only make you lifeless when living beneath Divine Truth. You have also been made distant from Divine Truth within illusions of unworthiness and inequality with which you know your neighbor. Upon these illusions you have built a faulty foundation for success and victory as you know it. It is within these illusions that you have come to know others as less worthy and equal to you within your victory. Each are a reflection of your suffering.

Your efforts to succeed and know victory are fueled by anger, hatred, and fear. These are the emotions through which you view your competitors, wherever you find them. You do not know the Love within their or your being, and you do not want to know it, as you fear it will weaken you. It cannot truly weaken you, however, as it comes from God. It can only empower you. All of your thoughts, words, or deeds fueled with anger, hatred, or fear of your competitors are the makings of your suffering. You must love your opponents even as you compete with them while honoring the talents you have been given. You must also defeat your neighbor or know your defeat within being the Love and Life God Is.

You have sought victory and success to do more than to honor the gifts and talents you have been given, and to do more than offer the services to yourself and others for which these gifts have been given. The illusions of unworthiness and inequality have brought dishonor to your gifts and service as you are using them to place yourself above all others within your earthly life. You have attached unworthiness and inequality to winning and losing, success or failure. Though there are differences in human talents and abilities, there are no differences in worthiness or equality between people, as God is present in all beings. The notions of unworthiness and inequality you have attached to success or failure, victory or defeat are reflections of your suffering. Your suffering can end when you abandon these illusions and come to know the success and victory of embracing your humanity rather than denying it.

The Control Freak

The Control Freak insists that he must have a great deal of control over what takes place in his life. Doing things the "right" way is of paramount importance as they reinforce his sense of control. He is greatly disturbed when things don't go according to plan, as this threatens his sense of power and control. His need for control often spills over into various areas of life, be they large or small. Relationships are particularly difficult, as he doesn't know how to share the control with his partner, nor does he understand the reason for doing so as his need for control must prevail.

Ego's Voice

I am the source of your intense need to control the world you live in. I foster your need for control, and when you don't experience it, a lacking sense of control. Your "control" thoughts, words, deeds, and feelings are rooted in my energy. You and the people who know you well have seen them often. You must use them to impose control in your dealings with work, play, people, yourself, change, problems, stressors, your health, and your feelings. You have learned to control these parts of your life rather than allowing them to control you, a lesson you have learned well. Control is your oxygen, and you must have it to ensure your safety and survival.

You must resist any of the control that others would attempt to exert upon you. Their control signals disorder, a loss of power, and a loss of control. You must exert control over their lives, as needed—and you, not them, are the one to determine this need. You are powerful when your ideas and choices carry the day, and you demonstrate weakness when they do not. You must hate the latter and avoid it at all costs. You must also dismiss the ideas and choices of others to hold on to your control, your power, which holds the utmost importance.

Control is more important than closeness in your relationships with others. Closeness represents a threat to your control, as it requires a need to give in sometimes and invites you to weakness, which you must avoid. Control is the means to your survival. Using your power to impose control protects you from all of the sources of danger. A world that is within your control is a safe world—a world that you can survive well within.

Spirit's Voice

Your intense power and need for control is blinding you and leading you to an illusion of ultimate human control which can only reside in yourself. An illusion in which you believe all must comply with your earthly wishes and demands. This illusion is disconnecting you from the Divine Truth within yourself and others. You are not able to be the Love, Life and Energy God Is while being consumed with your needs for control over others and life. Your illusions are not the source of your salvation, but of your suffering—a suffering manifested in the many times and ways in which you have imposed unneeded control upon yourself and others and life while failing to recognize Divine Truth.

You have not built a sanctuary with this control, but a prison—a prison comprised of bars of unnecessary control. You are not free to fully know the Love, Life, and Energy God Is within your being and others. To you, they and all of the other aspects of earthly life are threats to your control. Others are not free to know the Love, Life, and Energy within your being which is unseen behind the wall of control you have constructed. When you have awakened to Divine Truth this wall will be torn down and you will know the greater control available to you within Divine Order.

Your consumption with earthly control has also prevented you from awakening to the Gifts of Life and Creating Life. There is no meaning to be known in controlling all that occurs within your earthly existence. Only the darkness and emptiness that results from faulty expectations, needs, and guarantees you have formed within the consumption for control to ensure your safety and survival. The bondage of your control has brought suffering within the meaningless and purposeless existence you have known and have often put upon others. This suffering will end as you awaken to your Divine Truth and the greater meaning and purpose which awaits you beyond a life in which control is the only thing which matters to you.

The Exploiter

The Exploiter has a need to prey upon people or situations. She seeks to gain an advantage over others wherever the opportunity presents. She views all means of doing so as justified. Furthermore, she equates the accrual of any "goods," be they material or non-material, as a means to empowerment. To her, empowerment means having more than others. Having more than others have contributes greatly to her sense of empowerment. She perceives no limits or boundaries to what she may take and make her own.

Ego's Voice

I am the source of your need to take everything you want from whomever you want. You are entitled to everything that can further empower you. You must seek and obtain money, power, status, prestige, influence, and property in order to enhance your power. You must get them from friends, family, acquaintances, or strangers. Theirs must become yours. Anything you can use to further empower yourself must become yours. They are the means to your survival, and you must use any methods to get them. Intimidation, humiliation, manipulation, and deception are the methods you must use when necessary to ensure your survival. Ownership of anything you desire is your oxygen, and you must have it to ensure your safety and survival.

No one should have more than you have and certainly not those who are nearest to you. They cannot be more empowered than you are. That would be a constant reminder of your weakness and a threat to your survival. You could not live wanting what they have. They must come to know you as the strongest. You must build your fortress upon everything you can obtain from them. You must take what they own to build your fortress so they cannot build one, keeping them defenseless against your desires and needs. You cannot allow them to be as powerful or more powerful than you. You need not feel sorrow for their plight. They were only trying to take or keep what rightfully belongs to you. Their pain is the price they must pay for keeping that which belongs to you, from you. They were challenging or bringing your survival into question, and they must bear the consequences.

You need not feel guilt or apologize for your thoughts, words, or deeds. You use them to ensure your own survival, for which you are completely entitled. The skill with which you use them is a testimony to your power. You are justified in taking what you need for your survival. You are not your neighbor's keeper, and they are not yours. Their failure to ensure their survival is a reflection of their weakness and your power.

Spirit's Voice

The intense power of your humanity is blinding you to the Love and Life God Is within you and all beings. You also fail to recognize the Gift of Eternal Life with your consumption for ownership of earthly possessions. Each has been removed from your awareness with illusions of separation, inequality, and unworthiness with which you seek to fulfill your earthly life. These illusions have helped you to build a faulty foundation upon which your life rests—a life in which you have come to know ownership as empowerment. This ownership is the making and reflection of your suffering. It has often fostered strain and struggle within yourself and within the lives of others. You have lived great anger, fear, and hatred in the service of your ownership, which are all reflections of your suffering.

Your efforts to empower yourself through ownership of all that you want have been fueled by anger, fear, and hatred. These tools have helped you to know the suffering reflected in exploiting one's fellow humans with all of the measures you have used. They have distanced you from knowing and being the Love God Is, and from knowing the Love that resides in all others. Knowing the Love God Is will remove the need for ownership in the name of your empowerment and survival. Your entry into the Kingdom of Heaven cannot come with ownership beyond the Divine Gifts you have been given.

The Life God Is, is not one of ownership, but of stewardship. One does not seek to own what has been given to all, but to use wisely what has been given, earthly and Divine. Earthly ownership is only a notion in the service of illusions of separation, inequality, and unworthiness. There can be no true empowerment born of these illusions and ownership. Your life has been made lifeless within ownership of that which cannot be owned. It will be made full and truly empowered when you have removed this illusory need. This is when you will have awakened to the Life God Is.

You have been given the Gift of Eternal Life, which you deny every day—a denial reflected in your efforts to survive daily using manipulation, deception, intimidation, and humiliation in the service of ownership. You live each day as if it will end in your demise if it is not met with ownership greater than the previous day. An ending occurring mentally or emotionally, if not physically. You work to prevent this ending with exploitation of your neighbor, nature, and the environment, reflections of your suffering. The empowerment you seek within ownership has only led you to know the limits of your earthly life and blinded you to the Gift of your Eternal Life.

Illusions of separation are also the making of your suffering. Your thoughts, words, and deeds of exploitation in the service of ownership all reflect an effort to separate from others and God—a separation that does not exist, but which you seek within your suffering. A suffering in which you fail to know all has already been given to you within the Divine Gifts. You need only open your eyes for it to be revealed to you. Your empowerment cannot come from without, but only from within.

The life you know has been built upon illusions of inequality and unworthiness. It is a life in which some must have more and some must have less. Some are more deserving and others less deserving. These are reflections of your suffering. You cannot decide within ownership who is more or less equal or more or less deserving. Within the Divine Realm, all beings are equal and worthy. There is no determination of such things within the Unity and Oneness of the Kingdom of Heaven.

The Independent

The Independent has a strong need to remain beyond the influence of others. He clings tightly to his way of thinking, feeling, or doing things, often resisting or ignoring efforts by others—be they friends, family, or strangers—to assist him where needed, even when the assistance is likely to benefit him. If it wasn't his idea, he interprets it as an infringement upon his power and control. Good intensions and the quality of the help being extended to him are irrelevant to him. He equates receiving any help with weakness.

Ego's Voice

You must keep everyone at a great distance from you and to remain free of their influence. Your power enables you to obtain this freedom. Your spouse, children, parents, siblings, and friends, as well as those you know less well, must be kept at a distance. From this distance, no one can control you or imprison you. They cannot alter your thoughts, words, or deeds, over which you must maintain complete control. If they did so, you would become weakened and no longer free. Your freedom is your oxygen, and you must have it today and every day to survive and be safe.

Their thoughts and words will weaken you and must be ignored or when necessary rejected to keep them at a distance. Your survival and freedom depends upon keeping this distance. You do not need to honor the wisdom of any teachers or teachings that may come to you. It does not matter what aspect of life they are seeking to help you with. Ignore their notions of work, health, relationships, parenting, achievement, change, adversity, stressors, or conflict. You must not listen, and when necessary, you must push them away. They only seek to weaken you by narrowing the distance between you and them. They only intend to take away your freedom, which would threaten your survival and make you unsafe.

Those who would seek to join you by embracing your thoughts, words, or deeds must be rejected. They cannot have what belongs only to you. Sharing these aspects of yourself would require narrowing the distance between yourself and others—a clever way to take away your freedom. You must remain an island unto yourself, an island that no one can visit and from which you need not venture forth. You must live in isolation to know freedom. It is within this isolation that you can maintain the distance that empowers you with freedom and ensures your survival, today and every day.

Spirit's Voice

Your power is blinding you to the Love God Is in all places and within all beings. A presence residing within you but from which you have become disconnected with your illusions of separation and freedom. Your faulty human notions of empowerment built upon isolation and freedom are the making of your suffering, which is reflected in your failure to recognize your connection to all beings and the Love God Is within them. You distance yourself from the very things that can allow you to know a far greater power and freedom than can be known from earthly distance and isolation. These are reflections of your suffering.

You reside within an illusion of separation, not only from people, but also from God. This illusion leads you to believe that all needs can be completely met within the earthly realm. You believe you have no need for God, including the God that resides in others. Your failure to recognize the abundance available to you from within yourself and others is the making of your suffering. This failure embraces the notion that all of the answers to the challenges you face can only be found within the confines of your own human resources, another reflection of your suffering.

Your freedom is an illusion that can only bring the suffering of isolation, loneliness, and emptiness. No one is truly an island, as you are connected to all things. Your humanity may attempt to deny this reality in thoughts, words, or deeds, but the greater Truth will ultimately prevail. This Truth is revealed by the suffering you know from living within the limits of earthly freedom. Human needs place limits upon the freedom you can know within the earthly realm. It is when you can accept these needs and accept your connection to God and all beings that you will know no boundaries to your freedom. It is when you are free of your need for freedom that you will be truly free and your suffering will end.

The Bully

The Bully seeks opportunity to prey upon the weakness or perceived weakness of others. Each act of bullying adds to her sense of power. The more she can witness weakness within others, the more she can feel empowered. All strategies to accomplish this are welcome, be they physical, emotional, mental, or social. What she truly seeks is to gain as much distance as possible from her own sense of weakness. This is revealed most directly in how she often targets the most vulnerable of those whom she encounters. Bullying these people is safest as they are least likely to challenge her sense of empowerment.

Ego's Voice

You are to find the weakness in others. Look for it within their physical appearance, demeanor, lack of prowess, intellect, or social standing. Weakness of any kind—or anything you can make appear weak—will do. You must use any means to expose this weakness to yourself and others, which allows you to feel empowered. The weaker you can make them, the stronger you will be. The weakness of others is your oxygen, and you must have it. It is within your thoughts, words, and deeds that you have shown yourself and others that you are strong and powerful. Your strength and power makes you safe, protected, and able to survive well.

The pain and discomfort you have brought to others is of no concern to you. This is weakness, and you shall have no part of it. You must have no compassion for the separated, unworthy, and unequal. Compassion for the weak is weakness. This would also allow others to see your weakness and lessen your power. Enjoy their pain and discomfort, as it is a reflection of your power. Seek the weakest among you, as they will make your task easier. They can be brought to pain most readily and allow you to know your power most clearly.

Welcome those who would celebrate your power, and let them embolden you. Allow them to acknowledge you and affirm your power. It is within their company that your actions are further justified. They are your true friends, as they also seek to empower you. Remove or steer clear of those who question you and your actions. They only seek to weaken you and threaten your survival.

Spirit's Voice

The weakness you seek to expose is not within your neighbor but within yourself. Every action you take to mistreat your neighbor reflects this weakness. It reveals itself to others who recognize the desperate means by which you seek to be empowered. The mistreatment of your neighbor is a reflection of your suffering. The celebration of your mistreatment is also a reflection of your suffering, which is rooted in your own sense of unworthiness, inequality, and separation. Your suffering can never be diminished through the mistreatment of your neighbors. Mistreating them will not lead to your survival, either, only more suffering. Suffering will always come to those who live beneath Divine Truth. There can be no mistreatment in the Kingdom of Heaven, as all are worthy, equal, and One.

Those neighbors who would celebrate your mistreatment are not truly being your friend. They are as weak as you have been, hiding behind a mask of strength. They celebrate you in order to protect themselves. They will leave when their eyes have been opened to your weakness and you can no longer protect them. Such is the fragile nature of your power, because it is unreal. You have much greater power within your being than you have yet known—the power of your human and Divine Truth, which will reveal your strength and make you a friend to all of your neighbors. This power will remove any weakness so you may walk in Love and not fear.

You and those you have mistreated are in need of compassion. You are brought to the depths of your inhumanity by those who foisted illusions of yourself and others upon you. These illusions distanced you from your Divine Truth and the Divine Gifts you have been given. Let compassion come forth as you ask the forgiveness of others, forgive yourself, and forgive others who have misled you. Allow this compassion to bring you into a place of peace so you can journey forth in Love and not fear to the Kingdom of Heaven.

CHAPTER 2

Lower Ego Power Energy

Ego's Voice

You are to avoid the use of power and have learned that power will be harmful to you if you attempt to use it in your life, lessons you have learned well. It is safer for this power to reside in the hands of others. They can keep you safer than you can, help you to survive better than you can, and better know the thoughts, words, and deeds that can protect you. You must listen to them, not yourself. You must respect the power of others more than your own. It is within your powerlessness that you are most empowered. It is within your powerlessness that you are safest and can best survive.

The absence of your power will help you to meet the challenges and dangers that enter your earthly existence, whether they come from people, work, loved ones, achievement, change, adversity, stressors, or conflict. Stay out of the way and keep at a distance from these challenges and dangers—they will swallow you up if you attempt to take them on. Their power is greater than yours, and you must recognize this to keep yourself safe. Within the company and comfort of sadness and depression, you can avoid all that you fear, be protected, and survive. Your happiness resides in not encountering what you have learned to fear.

It is within the absence of your power that you must submit, follow, or know less than others. You must also know that listening to others is more important than listening to yourself. Listening to others, thinking what they think and doing what they do, is the means to your strength. You do

27

not know more or better than they do. Their way is right and doesn't need to be challenged or changed; yours does. You must mistreat yourself when necessary, knowing that you are less worthy than others, underestimate yourself, insist on doing things the way that other people want to do them, and to lack confidence.

Stay dependent upon those who are closest to you, be they your spouse, partner, or close friend. You cannot know as much as they do or influence them. Fail to communicate your thoughts, always give in to their desires, and do not expect compassion from them. They need to do most of the thinking so you can be protected in their wisdom. You must become as much like your partner as possible in your approach to life, so you can be a better person—your partner.

Love others more than you can love yourself, knowing that you are less important and less significant than others. You feel safest when you are meeting the needs of others while neglecting your own. Loving others, rather than loving yourself, is the means to your daily survival, making you feel safe, protected, and able to survive. Expect less love from others and see yourself as less deserving of this love. In doing this, you are not taking the love that others want, so you can feel safe. By empowering others with your love, you can experience the power of feeling safe. However, your love is less significant, as it is coming from you. For this reason, you know your love as less desirable for others, questioning its value for them and their need for you.

Achieve less than you want or can, so you can stand in the shadow of others and see them as better than you. You feel safest in this shadow, and this is where you can best survive. Know competitors as enemies who would seek to crush you, should you step beyond this shadow. You remain free of the consequences of loss or defeat by remaining in the shadow. Minimize or underestimate any of what you have achieved so you can remain in the shadow. You are safest and can survive best by believing in others rather than yourself.

You must readily believe or think what others would have you believe or think. Their wisdom can keep you safe. Venturing forth with your own thoughts and beliefs is dangerous and puts you at risk. Know their thoughts as unquestionable and infallible, unlike your own. You are most empowered when thinking the thoughts of others rather than your own. This is when you feel safest, and it helps you to survive well.

Fear all of the change that enters into your life and know that change is here to defeat if not destroy you. No good can come from change. Such good is only a disguise which will only make you unsafe and risk your survival. When change occurs you cannot manage it alone, and must seek the guidance of others to deal with it. Only through their power can you meet the challenges that change brings you in your health, relationships, finances, work, or family members.

View all losses, failures, or mistakes that occur in your life as threats to your survival. You must avoid them by failing to take any risks that could lead to them. You are safest when standing still and must not venture into these places which can lead to your undoing. When they do occur, you must seek the guidance of others, as you cannot manage them alone. Their guidance and wisdom will make you safer.

You are to embrace the sadness and depression that stems from your lack of power. They have helped you to escape from the dangers of living in the world. Depression and sadness have helped you to avoid the pain and fear you must negotiate in venturing forth from the shadows. I have also helped you to find happiness in the shelter of those who provide it for you—a shelter built upon the guidance and protection they have provided you. Safety is the foundation upon which you must know happiness.

Know that you are powerless in the face of all stressors that life brings to you. They are all larger and more powerful than you, whether they involve loved ones, health, work, finances, or relationships. They all conspire to defeat and destroy you. For this reason, you must keep at a distance from them, a distance that can be increased by refusing to partake in any of the risks that can lead to them. You must also seek the assistance of others when stressors do occur, as they know better how to manage them than you do. They can ensure your safety and survival better than you can.

You are to avoid all conflicts. Conflicts only represent an opportunity to expose the weakness of your thoughts and choices. You can only lose in a conflict, which brings your safety and survival into question. Conflicts are unnecessary, as others know more than you do. Even if you win within a conflict, you still lose. Winning means taking on the responsibilities that come with winning, and ultimately losing. Winning is a disguise for ultimate defeat and a threat to your safety and survival. You are safest when you lose and allow others to have the victory.

Spirit's Voice

Your existence is one of intense suffering—the suffering which comes from blindness as to who You are, who God Is, and the Divine Gifts you have been given. You have learned that you have no power within your *being, earthly or Divine. A lesson you have learned well and which is creating great earthly distance from God. It is within these lessons that you do not recognize the Love and Life God Is within and which surrounds you. You have also been disempowered by blindness to your Divine Energy—a boundless Energy that can remove you from your suffering within the empowerment of truth. This suffering is reflected in the illusions you have constructed and are impacting many places in your life. You do not fully recognize and feel helpless to end this daily suffering, which will end as you awaken and begin to hear my voice. In this awakening, you will know who You truly are, who God Is, and the Divine Gifts you have been given.*

Many illusions have brought the disempowerment and suffering you have known in your distance from yourself, Divine Truth, and the Divine Gifts. You have made yourself unworthy of yourself, others, and God with questions of worthiness which do not exist within the Kingdom of Heaven. You have made yourself unequal to your neighbors within comparisons of thought, word, and deed, which are unnecessary and irrelevant when you have entered the Kingdom of Heaven. The illusion of separation has led you to the suffering of loneliness and isolation when there can only be connection, Oneness, and Unity within the Kingdom of Heaven.

The Love God Is exists within your endowment as with all beings. A Love that removes all fear, hopelessness, and helplessness, which are each a reflection of your suffering. God's Love empowers you to be the Love you are in meeting all earthly challenges. There is no need to rely upon others in this task. You must only do what you have already been empowered to do within your service to God and all beings. Being the Love God Is empowers all of your thoughts, words, and deeds. The Love God Is within other beings will also recognize and honor them. There is no need to honor faulty earthly judgment from yourself or others, which lies outside of the realm of the Love God Is.

The Life God Is, is one of fullness and fulfillment rather than the emptiness and discouragement you have known within your disempowerment. It is one in which all of the possibilities which exist within and without can be recognized and realized. Your earthly disempowerment has brought blindness to the life that surrounds you, causing you to fail to recognize God's presence in all of life. Though God's presence is necessary for life to exist, this blindness has led you to fear much of what surrounds you. An ultimate fear, as fearing life is fearing God, when no such fear need exist. All which is good awaits you upon the removal of your illusions which have only brought you suffering. Awakening to life is awakening to God. Finding the face of God in the works of all beings and seeing the good works in what you have done is knowing that God Is Life. Without God they could not be done.

The Energy God Is always was, is, and will be, and you are of that Energy. However, it remains unknown to you within your needless disempowerment and suffering. This Divine Energy has always been available to you. It knows no limits and empowers you to experience all possibilities within God's Kingdom, even those within the earthly realm, which you have been denying yourself with disempowerment and suffering. Through Divine Energy, the hopelessness and helplessness within your suffering can be removed. As you awaken and open your eyes, the power within your being, earthly and Divine, will become known to you.

The Gift of Life has been given to you and all beings—a Gift you do not fully recognize, as your life has become lifeless. You are living a life of mere existence in which you are simply getting from one day to the next. Each day, a day to survive and not live. Daily reflections of your suffering. This life filled with emptiness, loneliness, and helplessness is not your true destiny. This existence can end as you grow to know who You are and God Is. The Gift of Life empowers you, showing you that your life has a meaning and purpose. You will come to better know this meaning and purpose as you recognize the service you are providing to all beings with your talents and being.

The Gift of Creating Life can be used to learn of your true empowerment. You have been empowered to create life with your body and mind through this Gift, a body that may be endowed with the ability to create earthly beings also endowed with the Divine Gifts that you have been given. Your mind can fashion wondrous thoughts, words, and deeds that can enrich what earthly life, and you, have to offer. You will know an empowered life as you open your eyes to the Gift of Creating Life that you have been given. This Gift allows you to see more of the life that is available to you—a life unbounded by the limits of the earthly realm. This Gift will deliver you into the Kingdom of Heaven as you grow to recognize it, freeing you from the boundaries and limits you have come to know in your earthly existence.

The Gift of Eternal Life awaits you. You always have been, are, and will be. There is no power beyond yourself to protect you and to ensure your survival—daily or eternal. Nothing can destroy the Love, Life, and Energy within your being. There is no need to fear that which is not possible. This earthly life is but a continuance of your eternal life, an opportunity for you to come to know who You are, who God Is, and each of the Divine Gifts you have been given. This opportunity is enhanced by the recognition of the service you are here to provide. The Gift of Eternal Life will provide you with endless opportunities to learn what you must learn to enter the Kingdom of Heaven. You cannot be left behind. Your entry will take place in the time and place of your choosing. This is when your suffering will end and your life will begin.

The Gift of God Within is present in your being. You can never be truly separated from God even within your earthly disempowerment. You never truly walk alone, though your illusions and suffering has led you to believe that you do. God is within all people, all places, and at all times. When you awaken to this Gift and stop separating yourself from God, your suffering can end. This is when you will come home and enter the Kingdom of Heaven.

The Victim

The Victim is entrapped in the notion that life has it in for her and that she is powerless to do anything about it. She can point to a series of large and small misfortunes as "the documentation" of her victimhood. She has talked herself into helplessness with thoughts connected to these events, validating her disproportionate sense that "bad things" happen far more often to her than to others. She often fails to recognize that the problem isn't really the problem, and that it's her helpless reaction to the problem that keeps her in the role of victim, a role that often provides her with a sense of comfort.

Ego's Voice

I am the source of your need to reside in the comfort of your victimhood. You are to know that all thoughts, words, and deeds from others are intended to harm you and must be welcomed. You must also be guided by all of the thoughts, words, and deeds you have learned to use to maintain your victimhood. They will keep you safe and ensure your survival. You must keep your distance from life and reside in the safety this comfort will offer you. Victimhood is your oxygen, and you must have it to ensure your survival today and every day.

You have learned to be deserving of your victimhood. It is within your thoughts and actions that you have become a victim. You must accept victimhood rather than to fight it, as your acceptance keeps you safest and allows you to survive. Embrace helplessness and hopelessness, which have become your friends and will keep you in the protection of your victimhood. These qualities will keep you safe from things that may endanger you. You need not venture forth and take risks that will threaten your safety. You must also reside within the protection of loved ones willing to enable your victimhood. They know better how to keep you safe. You must not lose contact with them, as this risks your safety and survival.

Helplessness is helping you to stay exactly where you need to be, here. It is not safe to envision life beyond your victimhood—a life filled with the unknown and with opportunities for failure, a life of endangerment with threats to your daily and earthly survival. You need to stay where you are and belong, which can best offer you the security of consistency, familiarity, and predictability, keeping you safe. You must also remain connected to your past. It is a known entity and can guide you, informed by experiences that warn you of the dangers of the present and future. You must remain connected to its wisdom. The world you must fear is the world you have already met and known. Do not be fooled by messages asking you to forget the past. They can only threaten your safety and survival. You must never forget the past. You will be kept safe by continuing to fear its return.

Spirit's Voice

The disempowerment within your humanity has led you to your life as victim, a life that cannot realize all that has been given to you within the Divine Gifts you have received. This life blinds you to the power of being the Love God Is and God's presence within your being. Illusions of unworthiness and separation persist within you to explain and maintain your life as victim while removing you from knowing your true meaning and purpose. You victimize yourself with your blindness to the Love God Is and your true empowerment, which are great reflections of suffering within your earthly existence. This suffering will end as you awaken to the Love God Is and God's presence within your being.

Within the Love God Is, there is no place for being a victim. You can only be helpful and hopeful, as the thoughts, words, and deeds you use are empowered by this Love. You need only to seek it within your being, where it has always been. This Love removes all fear. There is no need for fear to protect you from real or imagined threats. There is no need for illusory comfort in the safety of the victim's life. You need not fear or embrace the thoughts, words, and deeds of others to keep you safe. Your safety resides in awakening to the Love God Is and being this Love, which will fully empower you. It also resides in the freedom of venturing forth and awakening to all that has been made available to you within the Gifts of Life and Creating Life.

Your life as victim has taught you that you are only worthy of the evil that your earthly life has to offer, not the good. This evil can only exist when you empower it with earthly illusions of unworthiness. When residing in and being the Love God Is, you can never be worthy of evil and are only worthy of God. There are no questions of worthiness in your being, only questions of when you will awaken to it—an awakening occurring in the time and place of your choosing in which to enter the Kingdom of Heaven.

Earthly life as a victim has led to an illusion of being separate from God. You see yourself in a far different light than you see God. Your light is dim and dark, while God's light is bright and vibrant. You see two lights when there is truly only one, God's. You have created your perception of your own dim light and your sense of separation with your earthly illusions. When you remove these illusions and awaken to the Love God Is within your being, you will see only one light—the light of Oneness and Unity shared with God and all beings. It is then that you will realize that any separation was only of your own making.

The Martyr

The Martyr often sacrifices his own wants and needs so others can have theirs met. He has become convinced that he is undeserving of the good things that life may bring to him. Consequently, he gives away or rejects what good may come to him. He also perceives keeping good things or meeting his own needs as an act of selfishness, possessing a naïve and immature approach to giving to himself that fails to recognize the healthfulness of doing so.

Ego's Voice

I am the source of your martyrdom. You are to suppress your own wants and needs so others can have theirs met. When necessary, you must ensure that others are served, even when this service must come at your own expense. Your significance resides in your insignificance. It is within the sacrificing of yourself that you are safest. No one can then attack you for taking what belongs to them. You must be ownerless. If you have nothing, no one can take anything from you. Your thoughts, words, and deeds of sacrifice protect you and ensure your survival. Sacrifice is your oxygen, and you must have it.

All of your wants and needs are insignificant and undeserved as you have learned that you are unworthy. Nothing can belong to the unworthy. You cannot and must not serve yourself, nor can you ask or allow others to serve you. You must encourage others to see you as unworthy and undeserving with your thoughts, words, and deeds, living in denial of yourself and in the denial from others. This is where you can live most safely and survive best.

The wants and needs of others are more important than yours. Others are more deserving, and you must meet their desires, which you are powerless to ignore and avoid. Their wants and needs have become your earthly purpose. Failure to meet them will risk scorn and rejection from yourself and from them, which threaten your safety and survival. You must strive to avoid these threats through sacrifice, giving to others so you can be safe. You give for your protection and survival, and your giving must be endless.

Spirit's Voice

The disempowerment within your earthly being has blinded you to the Divine Gifts that you and all have received. It has also led you to an illusion of unworthiness that you know in your daily suffering, which is comprised of fearful and joyless giving in the name of your protection and survival. You give in fear rather than Love, and in this there is no true giving. The purpose of earthly giving is not your safety, protection, or survival. Earthly giving is the means by which you can learn of the Divine Gifts you have been given. Within this giving, you can awaken to the truth that far more has been given to you than what you perceive in your earthly existence.

True giving involves no sacrifice, because it is within this giving that one is always receiving. The two cannot be made separate when being the

Love, Life, and Energy God Is within one's giving. Sacrifice born within the illusion of unworthiness cannot make for your safety, protection, or survival. Giving up your earthly life with sacrifice will not ensure your entry into the Kingdom of Heaven. Do not ask of yourself what has not been asked for by God. Only give so that you can know all of the abundance which has been made ready for you.

Service to others can only come from Love, not fear. Service rooted in fear has led you away from God. Your thoughts, words, and deeds of Love will awaken you to the Divine Truth within your being. Awakening to who God Is and the Divine Gifts is your salvation. Walking in this light removes any earthly need for safety, protection, or survival. Being the Love God Is and giving in Love is the means by which you can awaken to your Gifts of Life, Creating Life, Eternal Life, and God Within your being. You have also been given great tools in the form of your talents, which you must use in giving with Love. When truly giving, you will come to know your earthly life's meaning and purpose and the greatest calling you can know in your earthly life—servant. Being a servant has no sacrifice when being the Love, Life, and Energy God Is.

The Dependent

The Dependent has significant difficulty exercising control within her life. She has little if any trust in herself and often looks to others for guidance. She questions her own judgment and decision making, often wanting others to tell her what to say, think, do, or feel. She is an excellent candidate for exploitation, manipulation, or abuse. People can readily come to take over her life, as she gives power away easily, not even realizing she has it to begin with. She doesn't believe that she is entitled to any power. She is excellent at accepting blame for things that were not truly of her own making.

Ego's Voice

I am the source of your dependency. You are to live in retreat within your thoughts, words, and deeds, failing to call upon them in your dealings with people and life. You must remain out of the way of others and avoid risking their scorn or rejection. Dependency is your oxygen, and you must have it. Your daily passivity and submissiveness keeps you safe and ensures your survival.

You have learned to let others lead as you follow, because others know better than you. You must know only blind acceptance and resignation, allowing you to reside in the wisdom of others. Living your life with the thoughts, words, and deeds of others will keep you safe and protected. You need not wrestle with conflict, change, or adversity. Let others be your guide. Your spouse, partner, or loved ones know better than you. Others can better manage your life than you can. You can survive best in their shadow, in the safety of your dependency.

You must know yourself as undeserving and unworthy of any of the earthly gifts that may come your way. Disown all of your wants and needs in favor of those of others, which are more important and you must know them in this light. You must also love others more than yourself. The more you love others and the less you love yourself, the better. This keeps you safest, giving you their protection. This is where you can survive well. You must also question the love that others may show you, rather than receiving it. Love cannot be received by the undeserving and the unworthy. Receiving this love will move you beyond the safety and protection in which you reside.

Spirit's Voice

Your disempowerment has blinded you to the earthly and Divine Gifts you have been given. You have replaced them with illusions of separation, unworthiness, and inequality, preventing you from truly knowing yourself, God, and the Divine Gifts you have been given. You live in the ignorance of these truths, which are the making of your daily suffering. Your suffering will end as you awaken to your Truth—a Truth that embraces who You are, who God Is, and the Divine Gifts you have been given.

You need not lean heavily upon others. All you need to empower yourself already exists within you. The presence of God and the Love God Is within your being have already infinitely empowered you. You have often revealed this empowerment to others in your thoughts, words, and deeds, but you have not seen it in yourself. It is within your slumber that you are suffering. As you awaken, you will learn that you are not weak, but strong—a strength that resides in being the Love God Is within your life.

Illusions of your separation, unworthiness, and inequality have come forth from your earthly disempowerment. There can be no true separation from God and your neighbor. God is always present within you and around you. You can never walk alone, even within your slumber. You can never be less worthy or more worthy in God's Kingdom. A false notion learned within the earthly realm and a reflection of your suffering. The Divine Gifts have been given to each and all. It is within the knowledge of these Gifts that you can awaken to your worthiness and end your suffering. You cannot truly be unequal to others, as God resides within you and all beings. There is no greater or lesser in God's Kingdom. All beings are different, but equal and One— This is the Love, Life, and Energy God Is revealed. A revelation that will end your suffering as you awaken to it.

The Depressive

The Depressive often experiences life as a place of emptiness, loneliness, helplessness, and hopelessness. His eyes are often closed to the meaning, connection, power, and opportunities available to him. If these things do not present in the manner required by him, they do not exist. He has also become unloving of himself for failing to remove himself from his depressive existence, a view he often believes others hold as well, thinking they blame him for his plight. He waits for good things to happen to him, as he believes he is unable to help them occur.

Ego's Voice

I am the source of your sadness and have made it your friend. This friendship is allowing you to remain at a distance from the privileges and responsibilities that life would place upon your shoulders, which would threaten your survival. You are to remain unworthy, unequal, and separated from them as this will keep you in the shadow where you can remain safe and protected. Keep yourself distant from what good may come your way as this will keep you safe. You must remain helpless and hopeless, so you can be safe. Sadness is your oxygen, and you need it for your daily survival. It is within the company of sadness that you can remain distant from fear.

You are to see nothing good in what you have done and what you have to offer. Believing in yourself would only place you at risk and threaten your survival, as you are not capable of protecting yourself. You are to believe in others, as they are better able to protect you, allowing you to maintain your helplessness and hopelessness. You have learned to see nothing good in what you receive and to be unworthy of it. A sense of self-worthiness would remove your helplessness and hopelessness, putting you in the dangerous position of having to do more to ensure your own survival. Keeping at a distance from others and life allows you to stay safe while doing less. You are to see nothing good in what surrounds you or to be worthy of what is good, so that you will not seek it and place yourself at risk. Your power is within your sadness, so you must put your energy into sad thoughts, words, and deeds, all in the name of your safety and survival.

You have learned these lessons well, coming to embrace loneliness, isolation, and emptiness, expecting and desiring less rather than more in your earthly life. This keeps you at a distance from the dangers life presents. You need not deal with people, who will only seek to further weaken you. Expect less from them, and do not recognize or accept their love as you are unworthy of it. You need not seek to achieve, as this will ultimately lead to failure. Do not recognize and use your earthly gifts as this will endanger you within any success which may occur. You must keep your distance from adversity and change by accepting it on its terms. This will protect you from these challenges, which can cause you only great pain if you try to meet them alone. You must keep your distance from all conflict and stressors, as they can only further weaken or destroy you if you engage them. You remain safest in loving yourself less and others more. No one can attack you for giving them more than you give yourself.

Spirit's Voice

The darkness of your deep sadness has distanced you from the awareness of who You are, who God Is and the Divine Gifts you have been given. This darkness has also led you into illusions of separation, unworthiness, and inequality, each a reflection of your suffering. As you awaken to the Love, Life, and Energy God Is, you will fully awaken to yourself—The You that is residing within the you of your earthly existence. As you awaken to the Divine Gifts and earthly gifts you have been given and learn to embrace them, your suffering will end and your life of meaning and purpose will begin.

God Is Love, and you were made from that Love, as are all beings. This Love empowers you to do great things in your earthly existence, removing the suffering of sadness, loneliness, helplessness, and hopelessness. These emotions cannot help you in your daily survival, rather the Love God Is within your being will allow you to meet all earthly challenges. It is within this Love that you can never be separate, unworthy, or unequal to God or any being. These are illusions learned within your earthly disempowerment which have served to deaden you.

God Is Life and you are here to be a participant in that Life. God has not forsaken you. Your life has a meaning and purpose beyond the suffering of helplessness and hopelessness that you have come to know. You have been given the Gift of Life in order to know meaning and fulfill your purpose—a purpose that you will know as you awaken to the Divine Truth within your being.

God Is Energy and you have this Energy, as do all beings. Within this Energy, you have the Gift of Creating Life. This empowering Energy will enliven and enrich all of your earthly thoughts, words, and deeds as you awaken to it. This Energy has awaited your awakening. It will allow you to know any earthly challenge as within your grasp, allowing you to meet all challenges with light and truth. You will know challenges as opportunities, not obstacles. Your thoughts, words, and deeds that stem from this understanding will share Divine Truth and create the greater life that awaits you. You are able to create the life in which you live.

The Underachiever

The Underachiever achieves less than she is capable of achieving, often significantly underutilizing the talents she possesses. This is rooted in her absence of belief in herself. She has learned to expect failure and can readily find it in whatever she is doing. She often avoids success and is good at overlooking or dismissing the successes she does achieve, often turning victory into defeat. This allows her to avoid the responsibility that comes with success and achievement—as this responsibility would remove her from her "comfort zone" of helplessness and ineptitude.

Ego's Voice

You have learned many things about your talents and not to use them. You remain safest when you keep at a distance from your skills while embracing the talents of others. Thus, you have learned to admire and encourage others in their efforts to use their talents, while remaining distant from your own. You know that others were meant to accomplish more while you accomplish less. Give up on yourself and thrive on the neglect of your own talent. The abandonment of your talents is your oxygen and will ensure your daily survival.

Your thoughts, words, and deeds reflect many things that you have learned about your talents. Most importantly, you are not capable of having talents that are significant. Because they belong to you, they cannot be of great significance. The talents of others are more significant because they belong to them. You have also learned that you cannot accomplish what you may seek to accomplish. To attempt achievement risks failure, posing a threat to your safety and daily survival, while removing the comfort you have come to know.

You must pay close attention to your failures and ignore or question any of your successes. Your failures best reflect your talents. Your successes are cruel tricks that will lead you into danger if you take them seriously—the dangers that come with success. You are safest in your fear of success and failure, so you must remain in the comfort of your failure to try. You must also listen to others who better know your talents, what you can accomplish, and what is worthy of accomplishment, particularly those who know your weaknesses better than you do. Trust those who will keep you from failure and success. They are the ones who will ensure your safety and survival.

You have also learned that others were meant to accomplish more than you are. They are the ones who are worthy of achievement. You must live through their accomplishments. This is where you can remain safest. Do not challenge or compete with them. Such efforts would intrude upon their right to accomplish with their greater talent, and a betrayal of your neighbor. In doing so, you would also betray yourself by failing to keep yourself safe and ensure your daily survival.

Spirit's Voice

Your disempowerment has led to abandonment of your earthly gifts and blindness to your Divine Gifts. You do not know that which you truly are and have been truly given. The source of your empowerment is being the Love, Life, and Energy God Is. Each of your earthly and Divine Gifts are to be used within this empowerment. Each of these gifts are to be used to enter the Kingdom of Heaven. Your earthly accomplishments and those of your neighbor are only reflections of the earthly and Divine Gifts you have been given and your willingness to use them. They have no permanent meaning beyond this reflection. Separation, unworthiness, and inequality cannot be attached to these accomplishments as they are meaningless within the Kingdom of Heaven.

It is within your disempowerment that you have been led to illusions of separation, unworthiness, and inequality with which you have made unnecessary comparisons to your neighbor. Each leads you to neglect your earthly gifts, blinds you to your Divine Gifts, and serves as an obstacle to the knowledge of your life's meaning and purpose. Your purpose is to provide service to yourself and all beings with the gifts you have been given. Within this service, you are now and always to be the Love, Life, and Energy God Is. This is your Truth.

An illusion of separation has led you away from being the Love, Life, and Energy God Is within your earthly work. It has made you distant from all of the talents and gifts you have been given to undertake this work which is a reflection of your suffering. A suffering in which you are unable to achieve with all that has been given and unable to recognize the service you can offer within your life's purpose. Upon awakening to who You truly are, who God Is, and the Divine Gifts you have been given, this suffering will end and your life will begin.

The illusion of unworthiness has distanced you from your destiny—a destiny in which you will accomplish great things, with the earthly and Divine Gifts that you have been given. There is no question of your worthiness, as within your being is the Love, Life, and Energy God Is. No one can serve as judge to your worthiness, even you. All are worthy in God's Kingdom. You cannot be made unworthy with punishment, anger, or disappointment from others. You cannot make yourself unworthy with fear or guilt. These are reflections of your earthly suffering—a suffering that will end as you awaken to Divine Truth.

An illusion of inequality has led you to unnecessary comparisons between your earthly gifts and those of others, leading you to abandon your own. These comparisons have led you to avoid the path of success and failure you must walk in your earthly existence. No one can serve as your reference, as you must walk your own path. Others cannot walk yours, and you cannot walk theirs. Making these comparisons reflects your suffering, as all are equal and One within God's Kingdom. The path to the Kingdom of Heaven is your own.

The Conformist

The Conformist needs to follow the lead of others. He does what he is asked or told to do, even when this violates his own sense of right or wrong. He leans upon and trusts others more than himself. Often he exchanges control over his life for a sense of belonging, acceptance, trust, and respect from the person(s) to whom he is conforming. His lack of confidence often leads him to believe others can do a better job of running his life than he can. Adolescents are often led into this dark egoic energy if they have had authoritarian or emotionally neglectful parents. Consequently, they often exchange control over their life for the belonging, acceptance, trust, and respect they can obtain from peers which was lacking within the home setting.

Ego's Voice

You are to think, feel, or do what others would have you think, feel, or do. To be led and to follow blindly if you must. You must disown your thoughts and choices, even when you know them to be better than those who are leading you. You are safest using the thoughts, words, and deeds of others to guide you. No one can attack you for their weakness, because they are not yours. Following is the source of your empowerment and your daily survival. It is your oxygen, and you must have it. It gives you the trust, acceptance, respect, and belonging you need, but which you cannot give to yourself.

You must follow all who are willing to lead you, especially those you have placed above you. You must follow whenever important decisions must be made, whether they involve work, family, faith, or health. These are the places where you face the greatest dangers and must be led by others. They can own the responsibility for any of your failures; you can give them your mistakes. You can live better doing things their way rather than your own, as your way risks rejection and scorn, which threaten your daily survival.

By following, you can avoid the challenges and dangers that will come to you in your daily life. The faces of these dangers will appear at work, in relationships, and within adversity, change, or conflict that comes to your door. You are safest thinking what others would have you think, feeling what others would have you feel, and doing what others would have you do. Each of these strategies will remove the danger you're facing and allow you to survive in the shadow of following.

Spirit's Voice

Your disempowerment has led you to follow others in the false hope of finding yourself there and being empowered by them. You seek comfort in living their thoughts, words, and deeds. This comfort is a form of suffering keeping you at a further distance from You. A suffering in which the illusions of separation, unworthiness, and inequality have distanced you from knowing who God Is and You are. Your suffering will end as you journey inward to You and to the Love, Life, and Energy that God Is within your being.

You have been given the Gift of Life, but you are ignoring and neglecting this Life by following others. You allow yourself to be consumed with the thoughts, words, feelings, and deeds of others while neglecting your own, in a lifeless existence that reflects your suffering. There can be no other life but your own. You can know no meaning or purpose from living within the life of another. You must live your life in order to experience the Gift of Life. When you know this, you will become truly alive.

You have been empowered to create your life. You need not live a life created for you by others to know trust, acceptance, respect, and belonging. There is no safety or survival when becoming someone you are not in order to meet these earthly needs. You must become You through the Gift of Creating Life. You were meant to be You. You need not hide from your earthly weaknesses or hide them from others in order to meet these earthly needs. You only need to transform them with the Gifts you have been given and the knowledge of who God Is. You are empowered with the Love, Life, and Energy God Is to create life, including your life, with your thoughts, words, and deeds. Within this empowerment, you will live your Truth, the only one which can be lived. A Truth in which you will receive all you need from within.

An illusion of separation has distanced you from God and yourself. You have lost yourself and seek to find yourself within others, a journey that is fruitless and brings you great suffering. You can only find yourself by going within, where God and You await. An illusion of unworthiness has led you to seek from others that which already exists within you. You cannot find your worthiness within the thoughts, words, or deeds of others in order to know trust, respect, acceptance, and belonging. You need not suffer within the faulty denial of yourself. Within God's Kingdom you cannot be unworthy. You can only awaken to your worthiness within the time and place of your choosing.

An illusion of inequality has led you to seek empowerment within the thoughts, words, and deeds of others, as you have learned to question your own because you see yourself as less than others. Your efforts to address this illusion are futile, as there is no inequality to be addressed. You are equal to all others, as there can be no inequality within God's Kingdom or within your earthly existence. All are equal and One within the Love, Life, and Energy God Is.

The Masochist

The Masochist believes she only deserves pain in her life, which can be inflicted by herself or by others. It is within mental, emotional, or physical pain that she experiences a sense of normalcy. The absence of pain, or opportunity to experience pleasure, are met with confusion, as they are unfamiliar to her. She often rejects these experiences due to their incompatibility with what she believes she deserves. The origins of her masochism are often rooted in her childhood in which she learned that she was only deserving of pain. Painful experiences keep her within the comfort zone of consistency, familiarity, and predictability.

Ego's Voice

You are to readily inflict pain upon yourself and to accept it from others. All sources of pain are welcome, be they thoughts, words, or deeds. You must endure and enjoy pain as the means to your safety and survival. You are safest when knowing pain in your thoughts, words, and deeds. Submission, humiliation, self-denial, defeat, and degradation are your friends. They will keep you safe, and you must keep them close at hand. Pain is the source of your empowerment. The empowerment of safety and survival. Pain is your oxygen, and you must have it.

You must know yourself as less deserving than others. This will help you to better know the pain you deserve. You do not want or deserve joy and happiness. They will threaten your safety and survival. Thus, you must see all that is wrong and nothing that is right about you and your earthly life. You must reject success where it may find you and embrace failure, which provides and confirms the pain that you deserve. You can gain no happiness in success and must see it as your enemy. You were meant to lose or know failure in all aspects of your life, and you must ensure this continues. Destroy success whenever you find it or it finds you so you can remain in the safety of its absence.

You cannot love yourself or allow others to love you. If you became close to others, they would try to give you their love. Reject the love others offer you, as it violates what you have learned and would threaten your safety and survival. The more they try to love you, the more you will need to hate yourself. You must do what they will not do. You remain safest in being unloved by yourself and others, this pain ensures your safety and survival.

Spirit's Voice

Your disempowerment has led to your thirst for pain—a thirst built upon illusions of separation, unworthiness, and inequality. These illusions distance you from the joy and happiness of being within God's Kingdom, distancing you from knowing the Love, Life, and Energy God Is within your being. These illusions also prevent you from knowing the Divine Gifts you have been given. There is no pain in God's Kingdom. It does not have a place, time, or reason. There can be no separation, unworthiness, or inequality to bring forth pain. The only purpose pain has in your earthly life is to let you know that you have been led astray by yourself or others. It can only serve you in this way. You cannot deserve pain from the thoughts, words, or deeds of others or yourself. There is no safety, survival, or empowerment to be known in desiring pain born within your illusions, only the suffering you have known.

You were meant to know the honor and abundance that God Is and You are. You cannot deserve joy or happiness as they are your ultimate destiny within the Kingdom of Heaven. Each of the Divine Gifts was given so you may know joy and happiness upon your awakening. The Gift of Life was given to know meaning and purpose within all of the abundance that has been made available to you. The Gift of Creating Life helps you to find your way to God's Kingdom and delivers you from earthly suffering. The Gift of Eternal Life removes any concern about earthly survival. You need only awaken to your Truth in the time and place of your choosing The Gift of God Within will guide you with Divine Truth to all the abundance which awaits you in the Kingdom of Heaven.

Awakening to your Divine Truth will free you of your need for pain and lead to your true empowerment. An empowerment that illusions of separation, unworthiness, or inequality cannot provide. Look beyond the imperfections of your earthly being and earthly life to remove your embrace of pain. Being the Love God Is can only lead to success even when you encounter earthly misfortune. Failure can shine the light and lead the way. See the greater good that is unfolding before you and others. Failure is not for pain, but for growth. The Love God Is was meant for you, and you must accept it from whomever or wherever it may come. It is often calling upon you within the loving thoughts, words, and deeds of others. God Is speaking to you within this Love, and you must allow others to be the Love God Is within their being. Rejecting this Love is rejecting God. Loving actions are human, but their essence is Divine.

CHAPTER 3

Lower Ego Flexibility Energy

Ego's Voice

You must believe absolutely in what you believe, think what you need to think, and know the truth for yourself and everyone. Your thinking is beyond questioning; you need never reflect upon it or seek the opinions of others. Your ideas, knowledge, attitudes, and interpretations are much closer to the truth. Neither you nor anyone else can question them. To question your thoughts would endanger you and threaten your survival. They are your foundation, and you stand firmly upon them. You are lost without them and would be unknown to yourself. You must reside in the safety of your thoughts, as they define you and everything. They are your guide as to how best to know, live, and survive in the world. You feel safest when others are also living according to your thoughts. You must find others who already live in this world—your world—and convert others who do not.

When necessary, you must help others to know the truth. You must always question their thinking and beliefs. They are the ones toiling in darkness, and you must help them to see the light. This light, your light, helps in resolving any and all earthly matters. You know best, and others must come to know what you know. Your light shines brightest, and you feel safest when others are coming to know your light. This affirms the truth upon which you stand. You must also view your conviction as a reflection of the truth upon which you stand. Your conviction validates your truth

48

for yourself and others. Those with less conviction are weaker and are only standing upon belief.

You must listen weakly to others and to be suspicious of their thoughts. New, different, or unfamiliar thoughts are likely to weaken you, so you must keep them at a distance. You are safest when thinking within the realm of what you know or want to know. You must also help others to think like you in their thoughts, words, and deeds. A world in which others are united with you is a safer world for you to live in. You are protected within this unity.

You must not listen to those who are closest to you, even if their intentions are good. They may lead you astray and cause you to lose yourself. You must ask them to find themselves within your thoughts, as they reflect truth. This is how you best show them love, and you feel closest to them and safest in their company offering them this guidance. You must also ask them not to change after adopting your thoughts, as that would violate the relationship, which can only survive in commonality, agreement, and unity.

You can love yourself most when embracing your thoughts and less when embracing those of others. The superiority of your thoughts leads you to think well of yourself. The weakness and inferiority of the thoughts of others causes you to think less of them and to hate them if need be. You must love yourself more and others less, as this will ensure your daily safety and survival. Others can join you if they are willing to embrace your thoughts. You can love them as yourself, as they pose no danger to you.

You alone know the truth of what you and others must achieve in life, knowing what is more important and less important. You must be the one to measure how much you and others have really achieved, as your judgment is superior to that of others in these matters. You must listen to no one else. They will only threaten your safety and survival. You are safest in using your own thinking, rather than taking advice or input from others.

You must not allow anyone into your mind. They must not freely add, change, or remove any thoughts within it, as doing so would endanger you and make you unsafe. Only you can make any changes to your ways of thinking. You must hold firmly to what you know, as it is the truth. Seek that which you already know, and which will affirm the truth you know.

You must look upon any of the changes that life brings to you with suspicion. Things that are new, different, or unfamiliar to you represent a challenge to the truth you know. Deal with them cautiously and with resistance, as they represent threats to your safety and survival, endangering how you know yourself and jeopardizing the life you know. When necessary, deal with these threats by bringing them into the truth you already know. This is how you are most protected and can survive best.

Life's misfortunes and stressors must be dealt with using the truth you already know. You must use your own thoughts or those of people like you in responding to them. There is no place for newer, different, or unfamiliar thoughts or the people who espouse them. They are lost in faulty beliefs that could only harm you if you took them seriously. They would only make your burden greater. You can protect yourself best by remaining in the realm of what you already know, which has always served you.

You must feel happiness only when all is in its rightful place as you see it. This order is in alignment with the truth you know. You must use anger against yourself or others when this order is disturbed. You and others must live by the truth as you know it, as this is the means to your safety and daily survival.

You must deal with conflict in a relentless manner. Conflict is a competition between your thoughts, which are rooted in truth, and those of others, which are rooted in belief, ignorance, and lies. You must lead others into truth and never allow them to lead you from it. Their way is the path of destruction and a challenge to your daily survival. It is best for you to keep your distance from them if they will not listen to the truth.

Spirit's Voice

Your existence is one of intense suffering—a suffering built upon the notion of an earthly truth that exists for you and all. You employ this earthly truth to know Divine Truth, though it fails to fully know the Love, Life, and Energy God Is within all beings. This earthly truth also fails to fully know the Gifts of Life, Creating Life, Eternal Life, and God Within that all beings have been given. These Divine Truths and Gifts have been narrowed and limited by your earthly truth and illusions. Thus, they remain unknown to you despite the goodness of your intelligence, intentions, and inner being, a reflection of your suffering.

The earthly truths you have fashioned have been brought forth by many illusions. Each has placed you at greater distance from God, preventing you from knowing You, who God Is, and the Divine Gifts that you have been given. Illusions of separation, unworthiness, and inequality placed upon yourself and others distance you from God's Kingdom. The illusions of earthly control and disorder have blinded you to the workings of Divine

Order, leading you to believe that all can be seen and known within the limits of one's earthly senses and mind with your truth. You must realize that there is no right way to know God within the earthly realm. You cannot awaken others to their Divine Truth with your earthly truth, even though you mean well. You can only encourage others to walk their own path home to the Kingdom of Heaven from where they came, a path marked with Divine Truths about who God Is and the Divine Gifts all have been given. All of these illusions have brought you great suffering, which will end as you awaken to them and come to truly know You, God, and the Divine Gifts. You will learn these Truths as you walk your path, which no one can walk for you and which you cannot walk for others.

The Love God Is exists in all beings, just as it exists within your being. It is available for use in all earthly works, including yours and your neighbors' as well as your enemies'. Only by being the Love God Is in your earthly works can you truly know God. It is within this Love that you can assist others in coming to know their truth, earthly and Divine. There is no place for fear or anger in your earthly work. When acting from these emotions, you are serving yourself and not God, a reflection of your suffering.

The Life God Is, is reflected in all beings. Each is a manifestation of God in their own way, and each having their own purpose. There can be no unworthiness or inequality in God's Kingdom. These are only illusions created within the earthly mind. Nor is there any place in God's Kingdom for judgment of worthiness and equality, as these questions do not exist there. They are only reflections of your suffering within the earthly realm, which ends with the awareness that all beings are given the Gifts of Life and Creating Life to do their earthly work. It is not for anyone to place judgment upon that work while failing to be the Love God Is.

The Energy God Is, is diverse, infinite, and beyond the realm of earthly contemplation and witness. This Energy lies beyond the limits of your earthly senses and thoughts. An Energy calling upon faith when one cannot witness it within earthly limitations. It is present in all places, at all times, and within all beings. There is no rightful or wrongful place for this Energy. It is present in those you may know as your earthly enemies. These enemies may not know its presence in you. It is the Energy you knew in the Garden of Eden, an Energy you knew before being consumed with earthly suffering and survival.

The Gift of Life cannot be known within the boundaries of your earthly truth alone. Earthly illusions have weakened the depth with which you can recognize this Divine Gift within yourself and others. Your life and that of your neighbor is much greater in its meaning and purpose and can only be known within Divine Truth. This Truth reveals all which has been given to you and your neighbors.

The Gift of Creating Life can only be known when one is free to engage in their own creation. A creation beyond the boundaries of your earthly truth. Earthly thoughts, words, and deeds constructed while being the Love, Life, and Energy God Is are in recognition of this Gift. Each person must create their earthly life with the earthly and Divine Gifts they have been given. It is not for you to create the lives of others within the thoughts and words you would have them use. Do not seek to remove yourself or others from this Gift with the imprisonment of your earthly truth. All have been given this Gift to embrace in Divine Truth.

The Gift of Eternal Life has been given so that all can be fulfilled that has not been fulfilled within an earthly life. God's wisdom is beyond the destructiveness and death often seen in the earthly realm. It knows the misfortune that earthly beings can visit upon each other within their slumber, and the misfortunes that can occur within natural events. No one can be left out or left behind in entering God's Kingdom. There is no need for earthly beliefs to ensure this will occur. All has been made ready.

The Gift of God Within cannot be cast from your being. You can only cast yourself from knowing this Gift. Your faulty thoughts and words have led you away from the Love, Life, and Energy God Is within your being and all earthly beings, causing you to focus on service to yourself rather than God. Look beyond your illusory noble intentions to know the suffering you have brought to yourself and others. Anger and fear are the best signs of betrayal of God's work. Only by being the Love God Is in your thoughts and words can you know the Gift of God Within your being and all beings.

The Authoritarian

The Authoritarian insists that his version of life is the only one that matters. His beliefs, attitudes, values, and ideas are seen as a reflection of the truth—and he insists this truth must become known to others, particularly to his children. He has an extremely difficult time listening to others, seeing them as offering something less than the truth. He often believes he is justified in the disrespectful ways he may attempt to bring others to the truth. To him, the end of "saving" or "helping" others justifies whatever means he uses. The children of the Authoritarian are often concerned with issues involving self-acceptance. This person continues to do to themselves what was previously done by the Authoritarian.

Ego's Voice

You are the teacher of the truth. You always know what is right for yourself and for others. Your ideas, thoughts, and beliefs are beyond questioning. They are the foundation upon which you stand, and you must use them to help your spouse and children or those closest to you to stand as well. They are what make you strong, and within this strength lies your safety and survival. Truth is your oxygen, and you must have it. Non-truth is your enemy and must be vanquished. You can defeat it with distance or aggression when necessary.

Do not listen to the words of those closest to you, like your partner or children. You are the teacher, and they must be the students. They cannot know as much as you do, as you know the truth. Thus, you must always question their thoughts and beliefs, as they are built upon ignorance rather than truth. Only when they know your truth can the questioning stop. Neither you nor they can question your thoughts, as this would imply weakness in your thinking. When necessary, you must deal with such questioning harshly so it will stop. Fear, guilt, anger, intimidation, and humiliation are the tools you must use to help others to know your truth and forget their beliefs.

You are being most loving when you help your loved ones to know the truth. They are wandering from the truth, with their thoughts and beliefs. You must prevent them from making the mistakes they would make by failing to know your truth. You must serve as their teacher for their greater good. Again, you must employ fear and its companions if need be to help them and to keep them safe. You may disrespect them if this will lead them to the truth and ensure their safety and survival. Your partner and children must always respect you, and if need be, fear you, in order to know the truth.

Spirit's Voice

The rigidity and inflexibility within your earthly mind has led to great suffering within you and loved ones. You have placed boundaries on earthly truth and who may know it, which places you at great distance from your loved ones, God and You. Your suffering has taken root in your consumption with the idea of an earthly truth that only you can know, leading to illusions of the unworthiness and inequality of those who believe differently from you, an earthly truth to which all can abide, and sensing all of the energy which surrounds you. This consumption has led you away from who God Is and the Divine Gifts that all have been given. All of your suffering will end as you come to know the Divine Truth that awaits your awakening.

There is no keeper of earthly truth, for it is as diverse as the beings within the earthly realm. The Oneness of Truth only exists within the Divine Realm and can only be known from awakening to who God Is and the Divine Gifts that all have been given. You can only be the teacher if you are willing to be the student. There is no Truth in teaching with fear, anger, guilt, or hatred. You are not being the Love God Is when doing so. Rather, you are being the fear, anger, guilt, and hatred that exists within you. All you wish to teach your loved ones must come from being the Love God Is. They will know and respect your wisdom for the Love it represents then, as the Love within your being can reach the Love within their being.

You are living in the illusion that you must make your loved ones worthy by helping them to know your truth. An illusion because you cannot make worthy those who are already worthy. You cannot make your loved ones worthy of you or God with your earthly truth. You can only teach them to awaken to their worthiness and Divine Truth if they do not know it. The illusion of inequality has led you to see equality in only those loved ones who share your earthly truth. A suffering in which acceptance and respect is a stranger. This illusion has also led you to interpret their differentness as deficiency, causing you to miss the diversity of Energy God Is within those who are closest to you, a reflection of your suffering.

You live within the illusion of witnessing with your earthly senses and mind all of the energy that can be known. You see no energy or truth beyond your earthly ability to know it, an illusion that has led you to seek to be the knower of the truth. This illusion has caused great suffering for you and your loved ones. You seek to be what you can never be. You cannot know their earthly truth or Divine Truth for them. You can only guide them to awaken to their truths by being the Love, Life, and Energy God Is.

It is within the illusion of complete egoic control that you seek to teach and protect your loved ones. According to this illusion, no earthly misfortune need occur if loved ones follow your truth. You seek to impose truth upon loved ones by "protecting" them in this way. Your desire to protect is noble, but it cannot be honored within your earthly truth. It can only be honored within Divine Truth when being the Love, Life, and Energy God Is.

Within your ignorance of Divine Truth you have obscured each of the Divine Gifts that have been given to your loved ones with your teaching and truth. Your loved ones cannot live the life they were meant to live with its meaning and purpose and they cannot create their life with your earthly truth. They cannot know their eternal life with boundaries your teaching has placed upon them and know God's presence within their being through your truth, only theirs. As they awaken to the Love, Life, and Energy God Is and they are, they will come to know the Divine Gifts they have been given. You can only serve them within this awakening by being the Love, Life, and Energy God Is.

The Racist

The Racist believes that race should have a significant impact on how people are understood and judged. She often views members of her own race as superior and those not of her own race as inferior. While racism is still widespread in today's society, she exhibits thoughts and behaviors more overtly than most people, and does not question their immorality. The Racist looks upon people of a particular racial group as lacking in their thoughts, feelings, or behaviors. This often serves as the basis for overt and covert discrimination against this group. She is prone to recognize or emphasize what is different about this group and fails to acknowledge what is similar to her own racial group. She also stereotypes and generalizes about members of a particular racial group while failing to recognize dissimilarities that exist within this group.

Ego's Voice

You must know the difference of another person's skin as their weakness, which covers and reflects all of the other weaknesses you know them to have. You do not need to look beyond the surface of their skin. The truth about them exists within your knowledge of them, and it cannot be challenged by them or others. You must see only their differences from you and none of their likeness to you. Their difference shows their inequality to you, their unworthiness, and their separation from you and those like you. You must use these differences to elevate yourself above them. Difference is your oxygen, and you must have it to ensure your survival.

You cannot love those who are different from you as you do your own. You must not bear witness to their goodness, successes, or gifts, as this would represent weakness in yourself. The display of kind thoughts, words, behaviors, or feelings toward them are also weakness, and they are undeserving of these gestures. They must all be seen as alike, and as different from you. You cannot love some of them and not others. Know them all as different so you can remain safe. Hatred and anger for them are your friend and will keep you protected. You must also teach this to your children for their own protection.

The love from those who are different from you must be discouraged and never accepted if offered. You must keep your distance from them, not allowing them to love you. Their thoughts, words, or deeds are only disguises that will serve to weaken you. Such gestures can only offer the illusion of being like you, equal to you, and worthy of you. You are safest when unloved by them, as their differences will not become your weakness. Their love will only weaken you and threaten your survival. Keep them as your enemy and you will be safe.

Spirit's Voice

The rigidity of your earthly mind has led to great suffering between yourself and your earthly neighbors. Within this rigidity, you are consumed by dark thoughts for your neighbors. The anger and hatred you carry for your neighbors in your thoughts, words, and deeds reflects your suffering. You visit the illusions of separation, unworthiness, and inequality upon your neighbors with your earthly beliefs and actions, which can only create distance from God's Kingdom. This has only brought you more suffering, reflected in the distance you live from Divine Truth. This suffering will end as you come to know that separation, unworthiness, and inequality do not exist in God's Kingdom, and that any earthly difference within your beliefs cannot make them so.

The Love, Life, and Energy God Is exists within you and all your neighbors, a Divine Truth that you do not know. You can only be the Love God Is at all times, in all places, and with all people. Earthly beliefs cannot change this. You cannot offer or receive love for some and not for others. Love has no limitations that you can place upon it. All must be the Love God Is to reside in God's Kingdom. Your place is waiting for you.

The Energy God Is manifests in many ways. All of the differences you have come to know in your earthly truth as separation, unworthiness, and inequality are the Energy God Is within all beings. Differences which manifest the Gift of God Within all beings. Those different from you can be no more separated, unworthy, or unequal than you in God's Kingdom. Earthly illusions cannot make them so. This Divine Energy has no earthly boundaries or limits. It can only be present in all places, at all times, and in all beings. There can be no distinctions within the Unity and Oneness of the Kingdom of Heaven.

The Religious Extremist

The Religious Extremist has a dogmatic approach to his religious belief system, viewing it as speaking the absolute truth about matters pertaining to faith and God. He often views those with different religious views as being removed from knowing or honoring God. The roles, rules, rituals, and customs pertaining to his religion are to be followed literally and rigidly. There is no room for alternative interpretations or modifications, which would dishonor him and violate his tradition.

Ego's Voice

You are to know that your way to know God is the only way. It is the way all others must come to know and honor God. Their way can only lead them astray and away from God. You must not listen to non-believers, as this can only lead you astray and endanger you. You must keep all that has been within the tradition and resist all that is new or different, as anything new can only lead you astray, weaken you, and endanger you. Beware of those within your midst who would alter the tradition. They are not true believers. The teachings and the tradition are your oxygen, and you must have them in order to be safe and to survive.

You must treat others who do not believe as you do with suspicion and scorn. They are the godless. Treating these non-believers this way, and harboring anger and hatred for them, will keep you safe. Let anger be present in your thoughts, words, and deeds. This will keep you safe. If necessary, you must destroy those who would challenge your truth about God. Doing so will honor your truth and God.

Those who do not share your truth must be known as separated and unworthy of God. You must know them as unequal to you because of their weaker beliefs. You must know the difference in their beliefs as disorder and chaos that threatens both you and them. This will end when they believe as you do. You must compel them to believe like you in order to be safe and saved. Those who do not listen will be damned.

Spirit's Voice

All ways to knowing the Love, Life, and Energy God Is are welcome. There are no right earthly ways to be the Love, Life, and Energy God Is. These Divine Truths have no earthly boundaries formed in the minds of human beings. The Kingdom of Heaven has no earthly boundaries or doors from which to enter. No one can claim to have the most complete knowledge of God, as God Is within all beings. One can only truly know God from being the Love, Life, and Energy God Is. All are One within the Divine Realm.

One cannot be made worthy or unworthy of the Kingdom of Heaven by earthly beliefs, for one is born worthy. They must only choose to awaken to their worthiness. God cannot be truly distanced from oneself or from others by earthly illusions of separation rooted in beliefs, as God is present and always in all believers and non-believers. Each has the Love, Life, and Energy God Is within their being. They must only awaken to these Truths. The Kingdom of Heaven does not follow earthly notions of order and control, which only place limits on your ability to know God and your Divine Gifts. These limits weaken your ability to embody the Love, Life, and Energy God Is.

All earthly ways of knowing God—past, present, or future—are welcome. Within the Divine realm, you cannot be enemies with those who do not believe as you do. This is only an earthly belief you have created. There is no place for enemies in your heart when you are being the Love, Life, and Energy God Is. Anger, fear, and guilt have no place in doing the work of God. No one can be compelled to enter the Kingdom of Heaven by another's beliefs. They can only enter in the time and place of their choosing. They can only walk their own path, and no one else's.

The Love Elitist

The Love Elitist has a rigid approach to romantic love and how it should be experienced and expressed, particularly between people. Gay, lesbian, bisexual, and transgendered persons are not welcome within her approach to love. She often seeks to impose rules and boundaries upon love, including rules about who are the "right" people to love each other as well as the right behaviors, times, and places for this love to be expressed. These rules and boundaries fail to recognize the unbounded nature of love.

Ego's Voice

You can only share your body and love with particular kinds of people. This love can only be known and shared between a man and woman. There can only be right words, right times, and right ways for love. No love can be known between men or between women. No one can violate these truths, for doing so would be wrong. These truths of love are your oxygen, and you must have them. They will keep you safe and help you to survive.

You must look upon those who do not follow your truth as confused, misguided, and sinful. You must question and revile their thoughts, words, and deeds of love, as they are on a wrongful path. There can be no true love between them and others. You need not honor their path, for it is wrong. Theirs is the path of chaos and disorder. Love between two people can only be found in the right places, words, and deeds. You cannot come to know their way of love, as it will weaken you.

Those who do not follow your way of sharing love must be looked upon as separate from, unworthy of, and unequal to you. This can only change when they come to know your truth. You must compel them to follow you by any means necessary. Insults, humiliation, and degradation are welcome. Thoughts, words, and deeds used for this purpose are justified, as they are for a greater good. You must teach them of their error, and you must not seek to know them, as doing so can only weaken you.

You must not welcome their overtures. These are only disguises that would weaken your truth. Rather, you must keep them at a distance so they can remain separate, unworthy, and unequal to you. This will keep their wrongful ways of love in a place where they can do you no harm. Their love is dangerous and can only make you unsafe. You and others will survive best by keeping them at a distance.

Spirit's Voice

The Love God Is has no boundaries. All earthly beings have it within their midst and can honor it within their thoughts, words, or deeds. There are no limits to where it can be shown and between whom it can be known. There is no right or wrong when being the Love God Is. The sacred act of unity between earthly beings has no boundaries in the Divine Realm. All are welcome to be the Love God Is within their thoughts, words, and deeds and only those who choose to be left behind are not included. It is beyond the harm that earthly beings may do within their blindness.

The Energy God Is comes forth in all manners and from all places. No earthly boundaries can contain it. It can only be welcomed as a manifestation of God's presence in all beings, a reflection of the breadth of Energy God Is. When you are being the Love God Is, you will engage in no earthly thoughts, words, or deeds that imply separation, unworthiness, or inequality. No one is more than or less than. These are only earthly illusions that reflect one's suffering.

No earthly being can decide another's path when being the Love God Is. The truth must come from within, and no earthly beliefs can shape it. No one can be compelled to love as another does. Thoughts, words, and deeds of anger, rejection, or scorn in the name of love are the reflections of suffering. One cannot be the Love God Is within these emotions. There is no chaos or disorder when being the Love God Is. Destruction or harm to oneself or others have no place in the Kingdom of Heaven.

The Sexist

The Sexist has developed and applied rigid beliefs and rules pertaining to gender. These beliefs and rules frame his perceptions, expectations, and values that relate to a particular gender. While sexist tendencies are still widespread in our society, this person displays them more overtly than the average person. He may not even question whether these thoughts and behaviors are wrong. He often ignores or discounts experiences of people of another gender that do not fit into the framework of his beliefs and rules. Often, he ascribes weakness or inferiority to people who are not of his gender.

Ego's Voice

You are to know your gender as greater, believing it is helping you to know the right ways of thinking, feeling, and doing. People who are not of your gender are weaker; their gender defines and weakens all of their thoughts, which only serve to weaken their feelings and deeds. They must be seen for the weakness in which they are rooted. You must not listen to them; they cannot be trusted. They can be of no help in your daily life. You must not honor or respect them, as they can only weaken you with their faulty help, threatening your safety and survival.

Do not condemn them for their gender, as this was not their choice. Only condemn that which is begotten by their gender: their thoughts, words, and deeds. Expect less rather than more from them, as their gender weakens them. Use your thoughts and words to lead them, as yours contain the truth. Compel them to follow when necessary so they can be made safe, delivering them from the weakness of their gender. You can save them from themselves. Ignore any of their complaints, as these are only coming forth from their weakness. They do not know better. You must only listen to yourself and those like you.

Let them serve you, doing what you will not do. Their weakness can only prepare them to do less, not more. When necessary, stand in their way if they seek to do more. This will keep them safe and allow them to know a purpose befitting their capacity, which will not weaken you or make you unsafe.

Spirit's Voice

All beings hold the Love, Life, and Energy God Is. There are no distinctions within the Divine Realm. There is no truth about gender in the earthly illusions of inequality, separation, or unworthiness that you have learned. These are only earthly boundaries you have sought to impose upon others. These illusions have caused you great suffering, brought about by the distance you are living from God and other earthly beings. The weakness you know is not to be found within others, but within yourself, in your inability to be the Love, Life, and Energy God Is while in the company of your neighbor.

You cannot stand in another's way, nor they yours, when being the Love, Life, and Energy God Is. You can only serve them where your service is needed. It is not for you to know or limit another's purpose or meaning. You can only offer support while being the Love God Is. Each person has been given the Gifts of Life and Creating Life to make their own way. Each individual must choose to know these Gifts and use them to know his or her meaning and purpose with Divine Truth.

You need not fear the thoughts, words, or deeds of another. They cannot weaken you when you are being the Love, Life, and Energy God Is. You can only weaken yourself with earthly illusions. There is no need for your compulsion to strengthen others by leading them to your truth. They cannot be made strong by it. This only dishonors them and is a reflection of your suffering. Let them serve you while being the Love, Life, and Energy God Is and you will know their strength.

The Ethnocentrist

The Ethnocentrist has developed a sense of superiority about her culture and ethnicity. She has developed notions that her customs, roles, and traditions are rightful and better than those of other ethnic and cultural backgrounds. This can contribute to distance and resistance to recognizing and respecting other cultural experiences and traditions. In extreme cases this can lead to attacks upon different cultures which are seen as competing with the world view of the Ethnocentrist.

Ego's Voice

You are to know your culture as greater than others, and the traditions you follow are the only truth, reflected in the thoughts, words, and deeds you must follow in honor of the tradition. Your tradition teaches you the rightful way for all to live. You must cling tightly to your tradition, lest you be weakened and forget the truth. Tradition is your oxygen, and you must have it. This will keep you strong and ensure your survival.

Those not of your culture and tradition cannot be your friend. They cannot truly be your brother or sister, as they do not know you. They must not be trusted. To embrace you as a brother or sister, others must know and live your culture and tradition. Those who do not are strangers or even enemies. You may revile those who refuse to know your truth. This will let them know their weakness.

You must not come to know the cultures and traditions of others, as this will weaken you. Their culture is unworthy of you and unequal to yours. You must keep such people separate from you and resist their efforts to have you know their culture and traditions. These are only disguises that can serve to weaken you. Your culture knows the rightful ways of thinking, feeling, and doing. Others can only lead you away from this truth. Their traditions must be questioned and challenged, as they are born of weakness and would weaken you. You may help them to do this. They must come to know and honor your tradition, as it is born of truth which makes it greater. You may compel them to do so, as this can ensure their safety and survival.

Spirit's Voice

All cultures and traditions are beautiful bridges when being the Love, Life, and Energy God Is. They speak the truth that one can know while residing in the earthly realm. A revelation of Truth within thoughts, words, and deeds when being the Love, Life, and Energy God is. Each serves as a path to the Kingdom of Heaven, in which all are welcome.

The ways of being the Love, Life, and Energy God Is are boundless. Each has been given the Gifts of Life and Creating Life, and all people have free will to use them in manifesting God's grace within their earthly being. No earthly being can place limits upon how others use these Gifts. No one can discern any true unworthiness, inequality, or separation of one's neighbor. There can be no stranger or enemy within God's Kingdom. Each person has the Gift of God Within. There is no rightful earthly home for God's presence.

One cannot compel another person to know one's truth. You must not revile those who know another earthly truth. The Energy God Is, is present and welcome within all cultures and traditions. They are not to be used as a barrier or sword to one's neighbor. Such treatment reflects the suffering you have visited upon yourself and others. Knowing another's path cannot weaken you. It can only teach you about the breadth of Energy God Is. You must honor all people for following their way to truth. Have trust, for it can only lead home to God's Kingdom when being the Love, Life, and Energy God Is.

The Political Extremist

The Political Extremist has developed a dogmatic view of how people should be ruled or governed—a view that is often ultra-conservative or ultra-liberal, though the former is more likely. Conservatism tends to lean far more heavily on traditionalism than progressivism, firmly rooted in long-established beliefs and values that may not fully recognize the current times and changes within the energy that comprises today's world. Political change that is inevitable is quite difficult for the political extremist, and he initially manages it with resistance and rejection.

Ego's Voice

You know the rightful way in which all beings must be ruled, and the rules that they must follow. The truth resides in the rules which have been fashioned for yourself and others by your ancestors. They must not be questioned by you or others. There can be no exceptions to these rules, as that would suggest weakness within your truth. Your rules are your oxygen, and you must have them. They are the means to your safety and survival.

Your rules will make everyone strong and deliver them from their weakness. Their power resides in their truth, which knows how beings must be led and how they must follow. The rules of others will only lead them to weakness and destruction. You know the order that others must come to know. You must teach them this order even if it is beyond their will. This order will keep you and everyone safe.

You must only listen to those who seek or know your truth. They will help others to know your truth as well. You must not listen to those who know another way. They are your enemy and can only harm you with their faulty beliefs and lies. They must be silenced so they can do no further harm. Fear is an ally and a tool you must use to help the non-believer to know the truth. The thoughts, words, and deeds you must use for this purpose will help you to share the truth with others. Neither you nor others must question these tools. Their questions are born of weakness, and honoring them would only weaken you. Do what you must do to be safe, strong, and survive.

Spirit's Voice

You can only lead or follow when being the Love God Is. One cannot rule in fear and be a true leader. Those who follow in fear cannot be true followers. You cannot be the Love God Is when fear has become your friend and others fear you. Rules and ruling born of fear call upon less within yourself and others. It blinds you to what is best in you and others. Fear cannot make one truly safe or strong. It can only lead to suffering, as reflected within your thoughts, words, and deeds. You must call upon that which is greater.

The order you seek cannot be found in earthly rules that attempt to impose complete earthly order to which all must abide. This earthly illusion has led you into chaos and disorder. When your neighbors must live in fear of you and earthly rules, only chaos can result. The true leader cannot be greater than the follower. There is no difference between the shepherd and the lamb. All must led and all must follow when called upon.

No earthly ruler or rules can limit the Love, Life, and Energy God Is within your neighbor. Earthly order cannot be imposed upon Divine Order—and for those who know Divine Order, rules written and abided by in fear are made weak. Divine Order will follow those who are not being the Love, Life, and Energy God Is within their earthly lives. Suffering takes root in those who freely choose to live outside of Divine Order, a suffering known in the fear within their thoughts, words, and deeds which have no place in Divine Order.

The Paranoid Person

The Paranoid Person has developed a significant distrust for all that is going on around her. She forms rigid, inflexible thoughts often lacking in the necessary social validation, which are intended to keep her safe. The only thinking she can trust is her own. Exposing herself to the thinking of others would place her at risk, while changing her own thinking would expose her to danger by compelling her to intuitively if not intellectually admit that she is not as well-protected as she had thought.

Ego's Voice

You must cling tightly to all that you know. The thoughts, words, and deeds upon which you stand will keep you safe and ensure your survival. You know all that can be known; nothing remains hidden from you. You must not question or change your thoughts, as this would weaken you and make you unsafe. You must not listen to others, as they only seek to weaken you. No one can protect you but yourself. This you must do by holding your own thoughts above all others. Distrust is your oxygen, and you must have it to keep you safe. You will survive best and be protected in your suspicion.

Beware of those who would teach you different thoughts, words, or deeds, even those offered in love, as they are only disguises. Fear is your friend, as it will warn you of those who would do you harm. They only seek to hide things from you and weaken you. Their difference makes them unequal to you and unworthy of you. You must know of them to keep yourself safe, but do not honor them. They would only harm, defeat, or destroy you if you honor them. Your ways are superior and will keep you safe.

Trust must only be given to those who know and live your truth. Those who do not try to change you are your true friends. They will not lead you into weakness and will keep you safe. If they stray from your likeness, you must let them go, lest you be weakened. If they betray you in this way, they have become your enemy and must be distrusted.

Spirit's Voice

Your fear is leading you from the truth, helping you to build the prison in which you reside, which is built of thoughts, words, and deeds born of fear and distrust. Within this prison, you cannot know the Love, Life, and Energy God Is that surrounds you. This prison gives you no true hope of survival, and reflects only your suffering. You cannot enter the Kingdom of

Heaven from this place, as within the Kingdom of Heaven, there is no need for protection. This prison is a reflection of your suffering.

Because you have the Gift of God Within your being, you can never be truly alone or isolated, as God is always within you. The Love God Is can empower you beyond any fear you have known. You must call upon it. Your connection to this Love, not distrust, makes you strong. It will help you to unlearn the fear and distrust of your neighbor which has weakened and imprisoned you.

The Love God Is resides in all of your neighbors. You need not fear them, only call upon this Love within them. The illusions of separation, unworthiness, and inequality you find in your neighbors can only weaken you. Your neighbors are not your enemy; you are. They are not consumed with harming you; you are. They are not the reason for your distrust; you are. You must become a true friend to yourself. That which is hidden has been hidden from you, by you. You are the maker of your darkness, and you can be the maker of your light. Your beliefs are keeping you from the Divine Truth—a Truth that will free you, empower you, and cease your suffering.

CHAPTER 4

Higher Ego Flexibility Energy

Ego's Voice

You are to believe what others believe, think what they need you to think, and know the truth resides in others, from whom you must learn it. You must always question yourself and never question others. They will lead you to the truth that you cannot find within yourself. Their truth must become your truth. They possess greater ideas, knowledge, and beliefs, which will not fail you. You can only fail by questioning them, which would endanger you and threaten your survival. You must stand firmly on their foundation and not your own. Theirs is built of stone, and yours of sand. You are lost without their truth and can only know yourself through them. You must reside in the safety of their thoughts, as they define you and everything. They are your guides for how to best know, live, and survive in this world. Thus, you are safest when living in their world. You must lose yourself in order to survive.

When necessary, you must help other lost people to know their truth. They are also toiling in darkness. You must help them see the light that others are showing you, enlightening them on any and all earthly matters. The people you've come to trust know best, and others must come to know what they know. Their light shines brightest, and others will feel safest when they know their light. You will feel safest when others know their light. This affirms the truth upon which your guides stand. You must also view their convictions as a reflection of the truth upon which they—and you—stand.

Conviction validates their truth for yourself and others. Those with lesser conviction are weaker, and they are only standing upon faulty thinking and beliefs. You must not listen to them.

You must therefore listen weakly to yourself and be suspicious of your own thoughts. You must not concern yourself with exploring what may be new, different, or unfamiliar in your own thoughts. You must keep such thoughts at a distance, as the truth does not reside within you. You are safest when thinking in the realm of what others know or want you to know. Their thoughts, words, and deeds must become yours. You are unified when you enter and become a part of their world, and you are protected within this unity.

You must listen intensely to those who are closest to you in order to gain their wisdom. Find only truth in their thoughts and words, and do not question them, as this would lead you astray and into darkness. Follow them so you can be close to them. This is when you are being the most loving. If you followed yourself, you would become separated and lost from them. Allow them to change you as needed, another way of showing your love for them and gaining their love in return. Your close relationships will survive best when you become most like them and least like yourself. Find yourself in your partner or other close loved ones.

You can love yourself most when embracing the thoughts of others while disowning your own. It is within the superiority of their thoughts that you can think well of yourself. The weakness and inferiority of your own thoughts would only cause you to think less of yourself—and potentially hate yourself. You must embrace others by adopting their thoughts in order to love yourself. Loving others more and yourself less in this way will ensure your daily safety and survival. Then you will pose no danger to yourself.

The truth about what you can and cannot achieve resides in others. They know best what you must think about your abilities and your potential. It is for them to tell you what is important to achieve and how much you have achieved. Their judgment is superior to yours in these matters. You are safest in thinking what others would have you think. You must not listen to yourself. That would threaten your safety and survival.

You must allow anyone into your mind who seeks to change it for the better. They seek to change the weaker thoughts within it, making you stronger, and you must allow them to do this because they bring you the truth. They are your friends, and you must treat them with complete trust, as they are the means to your safety and survival. You must honor them, as you are most protected within their truth.

When life brings change to you, you must deal with it using the truth that others know. They will guide you through these challenges with their wisdom. It is within their knowledge that you can best manage them. Do not look into yourself for answers, as they do not reside within. The changes will only overwhelm you, as they are unfamiliar to you and what you know. Your own attempts to manage them will only lead to danger and failure, threatening your safety and survival.

You must deal with life's misfortunes and stressors in the truth others know. The answers lie within their thoughts, and this is where you must seek them. You must trust in their wisdom, as their truth would not betray you. You must not betray yourself by looking within, where the answers do not lie. You would only find darkness and more failure there; you cannot be your guide out of the darkness. You must use the light that resides in the truth others know to guide you. This light will protect you, lead you to safety, and ensure your survival.

Happiness will be yours when you reside in the truth of others. You will feel safest in their truth and rest easy. The order you know from others has distanced you from the darkness and disorder of your own mind. Keep this distance, and you will remain happy. Lose this distance, and you risk fear, anger, and sadness, which will threaten your safety and survival.

Conflict is your enemy, and you must remain at a distance from it. It can only lead you to challenge the truth others know and lead you to your defeat. Your faulty thoughts and beliefs can only lead others to disown you in order to remain distant from your ignorance. You can gain nothing from conflict and could lose everything from it—including your safety and daily survival.

Spirit's Voice

Your existence is one of great suffering, built upon seeking earthly and Divine Truth only within others and not yourself. This suffering has often led you away from knowing yourself, God, and the Divine Gifts you have been given. No one can know or speak your truth for you, earthly or Divine. They only make your truth hidden from you when they try to impose their truth upon you. The Kingdom of Heaven can only be found within you. You only need to seek it there.

The earthly truths that have been fashioned for you have led you to believe many illusions. Each has led to greater distance from yourself, God, and the Divine Gifts. Others have taught you to place illusions of separation, unworthiness, and inequality upon yourself and others. They have also led you to accept illusions of earthly control and disorder. Each of these illusions which have led you to believe that all can be seen and known from the workings of another's mind. All of these illusions have brought you great suffering. A suffering that will end as you walk your own path, which leads to You, God, and the Divine Gifts. A path comprised of these Truths leads to the Kingdom of Heaven. Only you can walk this path; no one else can walk for you. However, you need not walk this path alone, as God will be with you every step of the way.

The Love God Is exists within your being. It is present in all beings, but you must know and seek it from within. When being the Love God Is, your mind and body are fully empowered. This Divine wisdom fully informs your thoughts, words, and deeds. It will lead you to truth—earthly and Divine. You need not seek it from another, as it does not reside there. The opening of your heart will lead to the opening of your mind to You.

The Life God Is can only spring forth from the meaning and purpose within your being. You were meant to be a manifestation of God in your own being. You can be no one else while being the Life God Is, and no one can tell you how to be the Life God Is. They do not know your truth, and they cannot know it for you.

The Energy God Is, is present in all beings, all places, and at all times. It has always been within you. You may call upon it for the great truths of thought, word, and deed that are meant for you. No other being can tell you how you must use it if they are not speaking to you in Divine Truth. This can only lead you away from your purpose and into darkness. You can only be your light and guide when being the Love, Life, and Energy God Is. The wisdom for this guidance will come from within.

The Gift of Life was given to you. It cannot be solely embraced by living the truth of another. No one else's earthly truth can fully tell you its meaning and purpose, which can only be known from being the Love, Life, and Energy God Is. You have been given the opportunity to be a manifestation of God's presence, an opportunity to enter the Kingdom of Heaven.

The Gift of Creating Life was given to allow you to know God's wonder within your being. You can only know this Gift within your own thoughts, words, and deeds. No one else can create your life for you. You can use this Gift when being the Love, Life, and Energy God Is. This will reveal the wonder within your being. This Gift will deliver you from the suffering that earthly illusions have imparted to you.

The Gift of Eternal Life was given so you need not fear death and know you are always welcome into the Kingdom of Heaven. A Gift which allows you to take as long as you need to know the Love, Life, and Energy God Is within your being. A Gift that knows the distance you must travel in order to enter the Kingdom of Heaven. You will enter this Kingdom at the time of your choosing, and you are always welcome there.

The Gift of God Within was given so you can know the sacred Unity and Oneness within all beings. You can call upon this Gift to refute earthly illusions of unworthiness, inequality, and separation, which have led you to seek truth from without and not from within. Being the Love, Life, and Energy God Is will help you to know this Gift, which you must call upon within yourself and within your neighbor.

The Child

The Child is an adult, but requires the guidance of others on a frequent basis. He feels lost without this direction and seeks it out rather than standing upon his own thinking. He trusts others more than himself to know the right things to think, feel, or do. Within an intimate relationship, his partner is likely to become a father or mother figure for him, replacing those who served this purpose when he was young. People experience him as quite immature and much younger than his actual age.

Ego's Voice

Your mind must be kept open so all may enter. It is the soil upon which others can build your truth. Their truth will always keep you safe and protected, as you have known since you were a child. You must embrace the warmth of their truth. They would not lead you astray, and you must not question them. Their truth will show you the right thoughts, words, and deeds to use. Find yourself in the truth of others, as this is where it resides. Their truth is your oxygen, ensuring your safety and survival.

The truth can never be of your own making. It does not reside within you. Thus, others must fashion the truth you will come to know, just as when you were young. Do not seek to lead others with your own thoughts, as this would only endanger them and threaten their survival. You are not to be the maker of the path, only the follower. You must not seek to grow by following your own ideas. Your growth can only come from the truth you know from others. Let them grow you from without, so you can grow from within. Let them guide you so you will not become lost. Their thoughts are the way of truth and the path you must follow. Wander off this path and you risk danger, threatening your ability to survive.

You must allow others to correct untruths within your mind. Find yourself in the truths that others are helping you to know. They are your teachers, and you can only be the student. Allow others to teach you to disrespect and disown your thoughts. They seek to help you by putting you at a distance from your own untrue thoughts. This distance will keep you safe, protected, and able to survive well.

Spirit's Voice

Your Truth can be found nowhere else but within. No one else can know your Truth for you, and you cannot learn it from them. They can only lead you to find your Truth when being the Love, Life, and Energy God Is. Just as you can only find your Truth when being the Love, Life, and Energy God Is. You do not need to build your Truth, as it already exists within you. You are the Love, Life, and Energy God Is. You need only to awaken to this knowledge and your Truth.

You are to be the maker of your path. There is no warmth or safety to be known in living another's Truth—any sense of protection is only an illusion. The thoughts, words, and deeds that are right for them are not yours. You can only find the right thoughts, words, and deeds for you by being the Love, Life, and Energy God Is. You have been given the Gifts of Life and Creating Life with which to seek and find your Truth. No one can own or disrespect your mind in the name of truth. This can only lead you from your path when failing to be the Love, Life, and Energy God Is.

Feeling unworthy of your Truth is only an illusion that reflects your suffering. You cannot be unworthy of the Truth that resides within you. You cannot be separated from the Truth by seeking it from within, that is only an illusion. You can only find your Truth by going within. The Gift of God Within empowers you to awaken to your Truth. The belief that you must make yourself worthy with another's Truth is also just an illusion.

The worthy cannot be made worthy from within or from without. Your worthiness rests in your being the Love, Life, and Energy God Is. You have also been given the Gift of Eternal Life so you may take as long as you need to awaken to your earthly and Divine Truth. The Kingdom of Heaven awaits your entry in the time and place of your choosing.

The Cultist

The Cultist has identified someone she must follow without question. She believes this "leader" possesses what she must come to possess in order to experience happiness and meaning in her life. This leader knows the right thoughts, words, and feelings to emulate, and she blindly follows this person so as to not lower the leader's credibility and her own access to the truth. She often wants others to know this truth as well in order to further validate the leader and her decision to follow this person. Her days as a cultist will be numbered when she begins to have questions about this choice and to see more of whom the leader really is. An awareness that the person she should be following is herself may then crystalize.

Ego's Voice

You must surrender your mind to your leader. This person's thoughts, words, and deeds will keep you safe and help you survive. This person is the knower of the truth and possesses supreme wisdom. You must give your mind to this leader to be safe. It is not for you to question this person's truth, which would risk your safety. Your leader will let you know this. This person's truth cannot be questioned, as they would never lead you astray. They seek to protect you and everyone.

The leader has been given special gifts that neither you nor anyone else can possess. This person shares their wisdom with you as a sign of love. The leader is raising you up with their wisdom and love. This person will lead you to be what you could not be otherwise, while delivering you from all of your weaknesses. The leader must become your god. You must also lead others to this person so they can be safe and survive.

You must distance yourself from those who will not follow your leader's truth—even those you love and who love you dearly. You must not listen to them, or you will be lost. They have been unable to make you safe or ensure your survival, even with their love. They have been unable to offer you meaning and purpose within their truth. They can only lead you from the truth your leader has shown you. You must challenge those who would defile the leader's truth, your truth. Your leader loves you as no one else has or can. Cling tightly to them so you will bask in their light. It is here that you will be safe, protected, and survive well.

Spirit's Voice

The earthly and Divine leader you seek can only be found within. You must be the leader of your earthly life. This leader resides within you, not elsewhere. Seeking this leader elsewhere only leads to suffering. The true earthly leader does not lead you to them, but to yourself. They can only serve as your guide while living their Divine Truth. You will become your leader as you also awaken to your Divine Truth.

Many illusions have led you to your earthly leader—illusions of separation, inequality, and unworthiness, which this false earthly leader has preyed upon. They seek to make you feel worthy, equal, and connected within their truth. Such leaders seek to own your mind with their truth, asking you to disown yourself and others in the name of their truth. They compel you to know their truth with fear or abandonment by them. You must now understand that no other person can be your leader by owning your mind with their truth. You cannot give your mind to another in order to know the truth, as it does not reside there. Requests by them to disown others in the name of their truth reveal the distance they are from knowing Divine Truth. You will not ensure your safety or survival in surrendering your mind, only suffering born from living at a distance from your Divine Truth. This suffering will end as you awaken to Divine Truth, within the time and place of your choosing, as you begin to hear my voice.

You have been given the Gift of Life to seek and find your earthly and Divine leader. This Gift will allow you to awaken to the true leader within you. A leader known within the meaning and purpose to which you have been awakened. A leader who will be known upon embracing the Gift of Creating Life within the Love, Life, and Energy God Is. A leader who can only be you as you have the Gift of God Within your being. You have no fear of abandonment if you do not awaken soon, as you have the Gift of Eternal Life with which to awaken to your Divine Truth.

The Loyalist

The Loyalist has blind faith in his partner. He often sees his partner as "walking on water," and he will think, feel, or do anything his partner asks of him. He sees his partner as beyond questioning. Questions would destroy the illusion he wants to have of his partner as knowing the truth, and he sees this truth as the means to his happiness. The loyalist wants to question and doubt himself instead, as this reaffirms the need to seek the truth within his partner rather than within himself.

Ego's Voice

You must find earthly truth within the mind of your partner. Your mind cannot lead you to the truth. You must lose your mind to make room for your partner, giving your mind to this more capable person. You will find comfort in the shelter of your partner's truth, which will protect you, keep you safe, and ensure your survival. You must question nothing about your partner and everything about yourself. This is when you are being most loyal. Loyalty is your oxygen, and you must have it to survive.

You must allow your partner to move freely within your mind. Let your partner guide you in all of the matters of life, providing you with the truth. Your partner would not mislead or deceive you. Cling tightly to the truth your partner brings you, or you will be lost. Allow your partner to compel you to honor this truth, knowing he or she is concerned only about your safety and survival.

You must not question or experience conflict with your partner, as this risks your safety and survival. Your partner's truth is beyond questioning, so do not question it. You cannot be yourself, as this would only be disloyal and lead to separation from your partner. The loss of your partner would be the loss of yourself. You would have nowhere but emptiness and darkness in which to go. You can know the greatest possible unity and love only by becoming and remaining one with your partner in his or her truth.

Questioning and conflict have no place in this unity and love. They can only threaten your safety and survival.

Spirit's Voice

Your partner is not the maker, knower, or owner of your truth—earthly or Divine. You must not seek it within them. The light of truth resides within, not without. The Love, Life, and Energy God Is and You are can only be found within. This Divine Truth exists within you as within all beings. Look near, not far, to find them. Illusions of separation, inequality, and unworthiness have led you from them. They are the making of your suffering.

Blind loyalty in the name of safety and survival is a reflection of your suffering. With it, you will never know yourself, only a resemblance of yourself in another, and a life of residing in the truth of another. You cannot honor others by living in their truth, or dishonor them by failing to live in their truth. Honor is the reward for living in your truth. Your partner's truth can offer you no shelter, only distance from who you are. When you have entered the Kingdom of Heaven, you will have no need for shelter, for the suffering will have ended as you have come to know your Truth.

The Divine Truth to which you must become loyal is within. A Truth shared by all but must be found within. Your partner can serve you by guiding you to find your own earthly truth with your mind. A guidance filled with the Love God Is. As your partner supports you in questioning and changing earthly untruths and illusions, the doors to Divine Truth are opened wide. You must also offer this service to your partner. This guidance will allow you to share great love and unity with your partner, as each of you embody the Love God Is.

The Gift of Life has been given so you may know your own meaning and purpose, not that of your partner. You have been given the Gift of Creating Life so you may journey to your meaning and purpose with your own mind. You are meant to be you and no one else, the maker of your own path. The Gift of God Within will empower you with the Love, Light, and Energy God Is to guide you along your path, ensuring that you will reach your destination. Your Gift of Eternal Life has been given so one day you will enter the Kingdom of Heaven within the time and place of your choosing. Your place has already been made ready for your arrival.

The Unloved

The Unloved approaches love as something that she can only receive from others, not from within. She experiences great confusion about what love is, and she often gets caught up in the distortions that others may impart to her about love. These distortions may relate to what love means, what someone needs to do to receive it, and who the right people are from whom to receive love. Unfortunately, this often leads her into dysfunctional relationships until she realizes the answer to her quest for love begins and is within.

Ego's Voice

You can know no love that begins from within. Love must be received only from others in order to know love. It can only be known in the thoughts and words of another, which must become yours, filling you with the warmth you cannot give to yourself. Only in the truth of others can you feel this warmth. This warmth will protect you, keep you safe, and help you to survive. To know this love, you must willfully give up your mind and rely upon the truth others know about love.

Their truth is the making for any love that you may have of yourself. It will make you worthy of love from within and without. You know no truth upon which to know love. You do not possess the rightful thoughts that can lead to it. They must teach you what love is and is not. They also know the rightful thoughts, words, and deeds to reflect its presence, and they understand the requirements for giving and receiving love. Within their truth, you will know the trust, respect, acceptance, and belonging that you have never known for yourself. This will help you to understand love and allow you to love yourself, which will ensure your safety and survival.

To know and receive love, you must not question what your partner or other loved ones tell you. This questioning will return you to the coldness of being unloved by yourself and others. Abandon their thoughts, and they will no longer give you love. Your love for yourself would then disappear as well. You would lose all trust, acceptance, respect, and belonging, in a return to coldness that leaves you unsafe, unprotected, and unable to survive.

Spirit's Voice

The Love you seek is within. This Love reveals itself when you are being the Love God Is within your own thoughts, words, and deeds. From this Love, you will come to love yourself, love all others, and be loved by all others. When others are being the Love God Is, you can recognize this Love in them. This Love has no requirements for how it is given or received. It is freely offered and received, with no earthly weight attached. It is present in all beings, and it has no limit, as its energy is Divine.

This Love empowers your own loving thoughts, words, and deeds. You are to be the maker of these reflections of Love, as the Gift of Creating Life allows you to do within the earthly gift of your mind. Others must hear your Divine Truth from you and you must hear yourself. Let them see the Gift of God Within your being, as you have been given the Gift of Life to be the Love God Is.

You are to be the lover of yourself from within. The Love God Is offers the trust, respect, acceptance, and belonging you seek in your earthly life. Illusions of separation, inequality, unworthiness, and earthly untruths have led you to seek this Love elsewhere. Dark places have led you into suffering, which is reflected in the distance you must live from being the Love God Is. The Love God Is has an endless warmth. You need not seek it elsewhere. You have been given your mind so you may know this warmth, in which there is no need for safety, protection, or survival in the name of earthly untruths. Your mind and the Gift of Creating Life will help you erase the illusions of separation, inequality, unworthiness, and earthly untruths that have led you to seek this warmth only from others.

The Silent

The Silent seeks to keep the truth within himself silent, a truth that often speaks of a painful past that he would like to keep at a distance. He may embrace the "truth" others speak and use it to cover up his past. Adopting the reality of others keeps him from needing to come to terms with his own. Questioning the truth of others can lead to knowing the truth within himself, which remains hidden behind a door he wants to keep tightly closed.

Ego's Voice

You have been led to the silence of not knowing your thoughts, words, and deeds, which keeps you safe and protected. Keep your distance from what may trouble you. Let these thoughts, memories, and feelings remain asleep so you will not know their wrath. Fear the truth within yourself so you can avoid it. The silence of your truth is your oxygen, keeping you safe and ensuring your survival.

You must remain a stranger to yourself and a friend to those around you. Become like others so that you need not become yourself. Do not listen to the whisper of the truth that may call you. Remain deaf to it, as it can only lead you into despair. Ignorance of your truth will keep you safe. Your truth is too dark and painful to be known. Knowing it can never lead you into peace and serenity, only to darkness and despair, a place where no safety or survival can be known.

Listen to and reside in the truth of others so you will not know your own pain. Seek truth within others so you can avoid the truth within yourself. You must cling tightly to their thoughts, words, and deeds. They are to become your refuge and your salvation. They will deliver you from yourself. Obey the conditions of their truth, as this will keep you safe from yourself. Do not question the truth of others, as this will lead to a reckoning with your truth. Their voice and truth will ensure your safety and survival.

Spirit's Voice

Your Divine Truth only exists within your being and it will deliver you from any painful truths learned from yourself or others. There is no pain or suffering that Divine Truth cannot lead you from into joy and happiness. Stand upon Divine Truth to transform and transcend your suffering and any painful earthly truths from which you have sought distance. God Is the Love, Life, and Energy present within all times, places, and beings. Seek this within, not only without. Divine Truth will lead you to the thoughts, words, and deeds of deliverance from painful earthly truth so that healing, forgiveness, and peacefulness can be known.

There is no truth that will serve you in becoming another. Your suffering will continue as long as you remain a stranger to yourself. You must therefore become a friend to yourself within the Divine Truth of your being. Failing to know your earthly truth offers you no refuge or salvation, *only suffering. The suffering known from living at a distance from your earthly and Divine Truth. To fear your truth is to fear yourself, a reflection of your suffering. Fear and truth are not to be made friends, but are enemies. Beyond the pain and suffering of fear is the joy and happiness to be known in your Divine Truth.*

The Divine Truth of your neighbor can serve you in learning your Divine Truth. When another person embodies the Love, Life, and Energy God Is that person can provide guidance in finding your Divine Truth and correcting your illusions of truth or reckoning with painful truths. Beware of those who seek only to convince you to know and live their truth or convenient truths. You cannot be made safe or transcend suffering by only following the truth that lies within another. Others may only serve as guides to knowing your truth from within, as you will learn to do for others.

The Puppet

The Puppet becomes what others want her to be in her thoughts, behaviors, and feelings. She wants others to "own" her life rather than owning it herself. This allows her to avoid or escape any personal responsibility for how she lives her life. Living in the truth of others allows her freedom from ownership, responsibility, and failure, an illusion preferable to the weight that she must bear in owning her own life.

Ego's Voice

You must find truth in others to guide your thoughts, words, and deeds. Allow others to carry the burden of leading you, and enjoy the comfort and safety of following. Let their truth be your truth. Build your successes upon theirs and have them own your failures, as you are only moving from their truth. When you work with their truth, you cannot fail; only they can as it is their truth upon which failure has occurred. It is within their truth that you can best live. Disowning responsibility and failure is your oxygen, which will keep you safe and ensure your survival.

Truth is an invention better constructed by others. Your efforts will only lead you into darkness and despair. Allow others to shape your expectations of yourself and other people, as they know better. Let them teach you what you must value in yourself and others. Let others lead you to what you must know, and keep you from what you must not know. Let them show you what you must feel and not feel. Adopting their feelings will keep you from needing to know your own or be responsible for them. You will also have no need for conflict, as you will become what others are. All of this will keep you safe and allow you to best survive.

Seek truth from within, and it will make you responsible for yourself and your life, for all of your weaknesses and failures. This will make you unsafe and threaten your survival. You do not need to be responsible for yourself. Let others own your life and the responsibility for being you. Look to them for the answers you need. When doing so, you cannot own failure, as it will belong in the truth of another. There can be no failure from within, only without. Keeping your own truth at a comfortable distance will make you most safe and ensure your survival.

Spirit's Voice

You were meant to be you, earthly and Divine. The You within is waiting to be known and lived. One cannot gain truth or know life through distance from one's own truth, only suffering. One cannot escape responsibility for their thoughts, words, and deeds within the truth of others. Illusions of separation, unworthiness, and inequality are leading you from who You truly are. You need not fear the truth, as it is built upon Love and not illusions rooted in fear leading you into faulty earthly beliefs of yourself and life. All of the answers you seek can be found within. The path to them lies in being the Love, Life, and Energy God Is and You are.

Disowning the Gift of Life cannot lead to life. There is no life with meaning and purpose to be known by living in the truth of another—only the false comfort of becoming another. You were meant to be You and no one else with your own meaning and purpose. The Gift of Creating Life has been given so you may fashion thoughts, words, and deeds that will lead you to know your meaning and purpose. A meaning and purpose absent when living the thoughts, words, and deeds of others. The Gift of God Within will empower you to take ownership of them. You need not seek them elsewhere when being the Love, Life, and Energy God Is. Their revelation will allow you to enter the Kingdom of Heaven where you can only enter as yourself.

You need not fear your earthly weaknesses, failures, and imperfections. They are opportunities to learn, grow, and move along your path home. They cannot be given to others, as they were meant to be yours. Fear of failure and responsibility are reflections of your suffering. The ultimate failure is the failure to be You. There can be no failure in being the Love, Life, and Energy God Is. This is your calling, and it will allow you to fully own your life, earthly and Divine, while entering the Kingdom of Heaven.

CHAPTER 5

Higher Ego Vulnerability Energy

Ego's Voice

I have led you to all of your fear, which is the foundation upon which many of your thoughts, words, deeds, and physical symptoms have been built. Fear is present within your earthly life and has found its way into many of your relationships and activities. Your fear leads you to seek to gain distance from the imperfection and weakness within you and surrounding you. Fear is your friend, and you must cling tightly to it. Its purpose is to serve as a warning of all things large and small, from within and without, that may threaten your survival. This fear keeps you protected and can ensure your survival.

You must be wary of those who surround you in your earthly life. You must keep them at a distance from your weaknesses and imperfection, just as you strive to do for yourself. Defer to their thoughts, words, and deeds so your weaknesses and imperfection will remain hidden. When necessary, reveal yourself only after putting great effort into hiding what is vulnerable within you. Always remain suspicious of others for their effort to find weakness and imperfection within you. Do not let your guard down, as they seek to weaken you with any evidence of vulnerability you have shown them.

You must be fearful in your relationships with those who are closest to you. This fear will keep you wary of any distancing that is occurring between you and them. Fear will let you know they are leaving you or that

84

you are leaving them, prompting you to find the source of this distance. Fear will energize the thoughts, words, and deeds you must use to narrow this distance, protecting you from the loss of these relationships.

Fear must also be present in your relationship with yourself. It will help you to rid yourself of your weakness and imperfection, so you will be able to like and love yourself more, and so others will like and love you more. When vulnerable, you cannot gain acceptance from yourself and from others. It makes you unsafe and unprotected, endangering your survival. Fear is the friend you must use to vanquish this enemy. Let it be your sword.

Your achievement must be fueled by fear. This will help you to use all of your potential while hiding any of your imperfection and weakness from others, and from yourself if need be. Achievement is an important means of distancing you from your vulnerability. It will also allow you to experience acceptance from yourself and from others. Success is your friend, and failure is your enemy. You must do all you can to know the former and to avoid the latter. Through achievement and acceptance rooted in fear, you can feel safer, protected, and ensure your survival.

Fear is the filter you must use to guide what must enter, change, or be removed from your mind. The thoughts and knowledge within your mind must be shaped by fear, keeping you mindful of the imperfection and weakness that is within you and surrounding you. They will help you to recognize this vulnerability and do what you must do to defeat it. In doing so, the thoughts, words, deeds, and physical symptoms of fear keep you protected and can ensure your survival.

You must also view the changes that life will bring to you with fear. It represents the unknown, and it challenges the aspects of you that are weak and imperfect. You can best manage change by avoiding or preventing it when fear gives you the cue to do so. When necessary, you must attack it so it will stop. Fearful thoughts, words, deeds, and physical symptoms will help you to resist change. This will keep it at a distance from your vulnerability. When change is absent, you are most safe and can best ensure your survival.

You must know your failures, mistakes, and losses through the lens of fear. They are reflections of your imperfection and weakness that you must avoid, ignore, or correct. Be wary of others, as they may also see them and hold you to account for your imperfection and weakness. You must use fear and its companion, anger, to distance you and others from each of them. These emotions will lead you to the thoughts, words, and deeds you must use within your earthly life to create this distance, which will keep you safe, protected, and ensure your survival.

Fear must be your constant companion. It is the fuel that guides your thoughts, words, and deeds, leading you to safety. Only when you are safe from your vulnerability can you know happiness. Safety guided by fear is the path you must walk to happiness. Your fear will not fail you. It will protect you and ensure your survival.

You must also use fear to deal with the challenges and stressors that your earthly life will bring to you. You must view each challenge or stressor as large so they will not catch you by surprise or overwhelm you. Your fear must be large so the necessary thoughts, words, and deeds will be available to defeat them. In doing so, your fear will help you cope with the vulnerability that weakens your ability to deal with challenges and stressors, bringing you into the realm of safety.

Conflict with your neighbor provides an opportunity to reveal your imperfection and weakness to yourself and others. Fear must lead you in your thoughts, words, and deeds to keep you at a distance from conflict and to protect you from revealing your vulnerability. When necessary, you must also use fear and its companion anger to defeat others who seek to expose the imperfection and weakness within your thoughts, words, and deeds. Use them to expose their own vulnerability so that yours can remain hidden from yourself and others. This distance will keep you safe and ensure your daily survival.

Spirit's Voice

Your existence is one of great suffering, in which you have made imperfection and weakness your enemy and fear your friend. Suffering in which you have been led to believe many earthly untruths about yourself and others. This has caused you to live at a great distance from Divine Truth and the Divine Gifts you have been given. You need not renounce your earthly imperfection and weakness to know your Divine Perfection and to enter the Kingdom of Heaven. You need only embrace Divine Truth and the Divine Gifts that have been given to you.

Many illusions have led you on a journey to renounce your vulnerability and blindness to the Divine Perfection of your being. Each of these illusions is rooted in the fear of your vulnerability. Fear has led you to know yourself as unequal to your neighbor. It has made you feel unworthy of your neighbor, or feel your neighbor is not worthy of you. It has separated you from your neighbors and made them enemies. An enemy to your earthly vulnerability. Fear has made you unequal, unworthy, and separated from yourself. It has led you to insist upon your earthly senses and beliefs as the source of all truth, earthly and Divine. You have been led to fear the unknown when it lies beyond the reach of your earthly truth. Fear causes you to insist upon earthly order alone as the only foundation for your comfort and safety. Earthly order, however, does not recognize the workings of Divine Order. There can be no safety, protection, or survival within these illusions, only the suffering you have known.

The Love God Is exists within your being and all beings. It is greater and more powerful than earthly fear. Your fear of weakness and imperfection, within and beyond, will dissolve when being the Love God Is. Experiencing yourself as this Love will reveal your Divine Perfection and allow you to embrace your earthly imperfection and vulnerability. You will then understand the suffering that the illusions you have sought for comfort and safety have brought to you. When being the Love God Is, there is no purpose or place for earthly illusions brought forth from fear.

The Life God Is, is a life of joy and happiness. There can be no happiness when living in fear of vulnerability. You are as you were meant to be. Learn and grow from your imperfection and vulnerability; do not fear it, as it was meant to exist within you. Learn and grow from others as they were meant to be. Be your neighbor's teacher and student while being the Love God Is. Within this service, you will know the greatest joy and happiness.

The Energy God Is abounds within your being and has no limits. It empowers you to engage in valuable works of thought, word, and deed at all times and in all places. These truthful works born of Love will make a friend of your earthly imperfection and vulnerability and lead you to know your Divine Perfection. You do not need the company of fear to empower you when living the Energy God Is. Fear can only weaken your connection to yourself and to Divine Truth, a reflection of your suffering.

The Gift of Life cannot be known in fear and suffering. Life is lifeless within fear. A life in which meaning and purpose are unrecognized. Do not seek it within fear of your earthly vulnerability and weakness. It does not require earthly invulnerability to be known. You can only embrace this Gift while being the Love, Life, and Energy God Is. This Gift was given to become You.

The Gift of Creating Life will deliver you from your fear and suffering. Your thoughts, words, and deeds born within the Divine Truth of your *being are the way to your salvation. They will not fail you, as they are the reflection of your Divine Perfection. There is no earthly weakness, imperfection, or vulnerability that Divine Truth cannot embrace.*

The Gift of Eternal Life was given so you will one day know Divine Truth and enter the Kingdom of Heaven. This Gift recognizes the journey of your earthly life, in which you wrestle with the fear of your earthly vulnerability. Your own free will determine the distance of this journey. This Gift has limitless time, allowing you to enter the Kingdom of Heaven within the time and place of your choosing.

The Gift of God Within is the Perfection you must seek. It lies beyond the fear within any earthly vulnerability you have known. Because of this Gift, you need only be what you are. The Love, Life, and Energy God Is, has and will always be within your being. Within the presence of this Perfection, fear of earthly vulnerability and imperfection, within and without, will dissolve. You will no longer seek what cannot be within the earthly realm, and then you will begin to enter the Kingdom of Heaven.

The Perfectionist

The Perfectionist insists upon perfection within most if not all areas of his life. He often focuses on what has been done less well or poorly while neglecting to see what he has done well, leading to the sense of not having done anything well. Often he cannot let go of what was left undone or done less well, having difficulty with moving on. This is often reflected in being self-critical and engaging in self-attacks. He listens poorly to the compliments others pay him, as his mind is focused elsewhere. He only rests when the undone is done well, but never for long.

Ego's Voice

You have been led to your perfectionism in order to ensure your safety and survival. Seek perfection within your thoughts, words, and deeds, as this is the path to safety. Let fear be your guide, as it will tell you when you are displaying your imperfection. You must have no tolerance for failure, loss, mistakes, or underachievement, which reflect your imperfection and threaten your survival. Fear will let you know this. You can only be alive when you are being perfect in your thoughts, words, and deeds. Otherwise, you will drift into the darkness and deadness of imperfection. Perfection is your oxygen, and you must have it.

Accept yourself only when you have been perfect. You must like and love yourself only when your thoughts, words, or deeds have been made perfect, nothing less. Only your perfection demonstrates that you have made yourself as good as or greater than others. You can only feel safely connected to others within your perfection. Within perfection, things are the way they were meant to be, allowing you to know safety and survival. Imperfection within yourself will lead to danger, and you must fear it.

You can only be accepted by others when achieving perfection. You must demonstrate perfection to hide from others what they must not see. Their witness to your imperfection will make you unsafe and vulnerable. Do not trust that others will accept you as you are. You are vulnerable to those who would see your weaknesses and imperfections, so keep them distant from them. Your thoughts, words, and deeds must remain hidden until you have made them perfect. Only perfection will make you liked and loved by others. It is only within your perfection that they can see you the way you need them to see you and see yourself.

Spirit's Voice

Your Perfection lies within your Divinity, within being the Love, Life, and Energy God Is. You cannot make yourself perfect, as this Divinity is the truest expression of who You are. You can only awaken to your Perfection. Earthly perfection cannot lead you to it, as it does not exist within the earthly realm. This is only an illusion, and the source of great suffering. Illusions of earthly perfection cannot make you worthy, equal, or connected to others—nor they to you. These efforts are only reflections of your suffering. Earthly perfection will not make you safe or ensure your survival. It has only imprisoned you, a reflection of your suffering.

You cannot truly love yourself when struggling to achieve earthly perfection. No condition need be met for love and acceptance within Divine Truth. Love yourself and let others love you for who you are, not for whom you must become. Your imperfection is your friend; you must not make it your enemy. You need not remove it to love yourself or to be loved by others. You must embrace all of your earthly imperfection with Divine Truth. Seek *to learn and grow from your earthly imperfection while being the Love, Life, and Energy God Is. Do not be judged in fear by yourself or others, as there can be no judge in the Kingdom of Heaven.*

The energy within your earthly perfection is destructive, as it is built upon fear. It has blinded you to your Divine Perfection, which rests upon the Love within your being. Your life has been made lifeless, consumed with fear—a reflection of your suffering. You have endangered yourself with fear of your own making. Do not hide from yourself or others with your illusions of earthly perfection. You can only know and live your Perfection within Love, not fear. Abandon your fear with Love so you can awaken to your Perfection.

The Overachiever

The Overachiever works very hard to achieve, often putting forth an abnormal or superhuman amount of effort to achieve. Often, this leads her to neglect other important areas of life such as health, family, or recreation. She is often driven by feelings of insecurity and unworthiness that she is trying to remove with her achievement. She may also be driven by the need to prove something to someone or earn their approval and acceptance, which never seems to be forthcoming. While this approval and acceptance is absent within her, she can never truly know it from without or learn that it is unnecessary.

Ego's Voice

You must strive to achieve in order to remove any of your vulnerability. Proving your abilities will distance you from your vulnerability. Let fear motivate you in developing your abilities so your work will be superior to that of others. Let fear be present within the thoughts, words, and deeds with which you seek to achieve. Do not rest until you have separated yourself from others and have risen above them. Achievement is your oxygen, and you must have it. This is where you are safe and can survive best.

Your accomplishments are the basis upon which you must judge and love yourself. Through them, you will know acceptance and worthiness from yourself and others. You must know yourself by the work you do and your accomplishments. Your purpose resides within your earthly achievement, and this achievement also allows you to truly live. You must avoid failure at all costs, as failure makes you vulnerable and unsafe, threatening your survival and making you lifeless. Do not rest or take part in play, as this will distance you from accomplishment by distracting you and making you vulnerable.

You must see your competitors as your enemies. They seek to take what you must have. See them through the lens of fear, and vanquish them with your achievement. Seek the acknowledgment of others at all times, as this will affirm your worthiness and let you know that others are unequal to you. Look down upon, question, or dishonor their accomplishments, as this will make you stronger and less vulnerable. It is within your accomplishments and the absence of their accomplishment that you are safe, protected, and will ensure your survival.

Spirit's Voice

You have been given your talents to be the Love, Life, and Energy God Is. These tools will help you to learn your purpose, earthly and Divine. You must use these tools wisely in service to yourself and others. You cannot raise yourself above others or lower them with these tools, as no one is greater or lesser than anyone else in God's Kingdom. You cannot make yourself worthy or others less worthy with your achievement, as all were born worthy. You have been given earthly gifts and Divine Gifts to do great works with your thoughts, words, and deeds—works born of Divine Truth. You are meant to be a reflection of Divine Truth within the time and place of your choosing.

Your earthly gifts were given to be used with Love, not fear. Work with them in joy. Do not fear your earthly vulnerability as there is no vulnerability to be feared within Divine Truth. Earthly achievement and purpose is diminished within fear. Do not make your neighbor your enemy through your efforts to achieve, which would only be a reflection of your suffering. Do not fear your earthly vulnerability as it will give you strength within the acceptance of who you truly are, both earthly and Divine. God is present within you. There is no need for fear.

Let failure be your teacher, not your enemy, as it will guide you. In failure, you can learn of your humanity. It will let you know how far you have traveled and how far you must go. It will allow you to celebrate your earthly successes and victories. Do not fear it. Do not let others teach you to fear it. Embrace it with compassion when you find it within yourself and others. Let the Divine Truth of your being heal your failure within your thoughts, words, and deeds.

The High-Maintenance Partner

The High-Maintenance Partner requires frequent acknowledgment, acceptance, and approval from his partner. There are lots of feelings of insecurity and self-doubt that drive him toward these needs. He is very sensitive to signs of rejection and can readily find them in his partner's thoughts, words, and deeds, even those that are quite normal and innocent. Often, his partner may have to engage in some form of damage control to help him know he is still loved and has not been abandoned.

Ego's Voice

You have been led to your partner, who will ensure your safety and survival. Being with your partner makes you less vulnerable, so you do not have to walk alone in fear. You must remain closely attached to your partner to experience connection to him or her. Fear must shape the thoughts, words, and deeds used within this relationship. You are lifeless without the relationship, so you must do anything necessary to keep it. Losing this attachment would make you unsafe and threaten your survival. Your world would be empty without your partner. Attachment is your oxygen, and you must have it.

Seek the attention, affection, and approval of your partner at all times. Ask your partner to raise you up in these ways. Your partner's acceptance allows you to accept yourself. Know your worth from your attachment to your partner, for without your partner, you are nothing. Only through your partner can you know your worth. When necessary, elevate yourself above your partner and have him or her adore you. Remind yourself and your partner of the great fortune of your presence within his or her life. Demean your partner when he or she has not appropriately honored you to acknowledge your worth.

Be wary and always looks for signs that your partner may be leaving or abandoning you. Find them within their thoughts, words, and deeds. Question your partner when necessary to prevent him or her from wandering from you. Ask your partner often to prove his or her love for you. Use fear or guilt when needed to keep your partner close. Let your partner know how much you need him or her. Tell your partner what he or she owes you, and express your inability to live without him or her. Your partner's loss would threaten your survival, and you must do all you can to prevent it.

Spirit's Voice

The foundation of your self-acceptance cannot be built upon acceptance by others. Acceptance must come from within. The foundation for this acceptance already exists, and you must only find it. You are already the Love, Life, and Energy God Is. Divine Truth reflected within your thoughts, words, and deeds is the path to acceptance, on which there are no longer questions born of fear. Fear cannot lead you to acceptance from your partner. It will only bring suffering to you and your loved one.

Do not ask of your partner what is not of their doing. It is not their task to remove your fear and weakness. Embrace your own weakness with Divine Truth and you need not fear it. Do not ask your partner to remain obligated to you in fear or guilt. Fear creates separation rather than connection, which would bring lifelessness and suffering to your relationship. Do not seek to raise or know your worth from your partner's gestures of validation, as your worth already exists and can never be diminished. This awareness can only be removed with fear. Fear present within faulty thoughts, words, and deeds are reflections of your suffering.

Seek a connection with yourself upon which to build one with your partner. Know acceptance from within so you will truly know it from without. Use the Gift of Creating Life to build a connection to yourself and partner with Love, not fear. Let the Love within each of you be joined in your thoughts, words, and deeds. Let your love be free and without weight, so it may grow and enfold you with your partner.

The Stressed-Out Person

The Stressed-Out Person is prone to find danger lurking behind every corner. She is an expert in finding things to worry about. This includes any perceived threats, large or small, real or imagined, currently occurring or yet to occur. She becomes upset easily, experiences intense feelings of anxiety or anger, and remains upset even after she or someone else has dealt with the threat. She has great difficulty letting go of things and moving on. Her normal state of experience is feeling stressed, and she seems to be lost when not in this state.

Ego's Voice

You have been led to your discomfort in order to ensure your safety and survival. Listen closely to your body, as it will always tell you when danger is near. Do not play, as you must always work to remain safe and protected. Look constantly to find the challenges that surround, await, and threaten you. You will find them in people, places, activities, and objects. Find them where they are hiding before they find you. All are opportunities to reveal your weakness, which you must not allow. Weakness from which you must keep your distance. Stress is your oxygen, and you must have it. It is the means to your safety and survival.

You must know all challenges as a threat to your daily life—an enemy serving as a means to your destruction. Look at them through the lens of fear, and you will not be caught off guard. Do not take your eyes off them even when you sleep, lest they gain the upper hand. Do not rest or seek laughter or enjoyment, as this will distract you and make you unsafe. Know all challenges as large, and you will not be taken by surprise. View happiness with suspicion, as it will make you unsafe. Let fear fill your thoughts, words, and deeds when answering challenges. Seek to destroy them before they destroy you.

Challenges unmet and undefeated will bring chaos and disorder into your life. These moments without consistency, certainty, or familiarity will destroy you. They will lead you to know your unworthiness and inequality. Act quickly and decisively in response to them. Remain on guard after they have passed in order to prevent their return. When necessary, distance yourself from these challenges with any means that will defeat them and give you comfort. This will keep you safe and ensure your survival.

Spirit's Voice

All earthly challenges can be embraced within Divine Truth. You can never walk alone in answering them. They are to be known as your friend, not your enemy—opportunities for growth, not destruction. Use them to know your weaknesses, and to work with your weaknesses in Divine Truth. Thoughts, words, and deeds born of fear will not deliver you from your suffering. They can only imprison you within it. Living with fear doesn't help you survive; it makes you lifeless—a reflection of your suffering.

Your body has become your enemy rather than your friend. The illusions you have learned make it a tool of fear rather than love—and you listen to it with fear, not Love. You need not alter your body with earthly aides to defeat challenges or overcome fear. Do not use them to hide from your weakness and yourself. Doing so reflects your suffering. Rather, honor and celebrate your body in Love, as it is serving you within your earthly life. It is with Love that you must know and cleanse yourself of fear.

You live in the illusion of separation from You, which is guided by fear. This illusion will end as you learn your Divine Truth. Working through the challenges you face with Love will lead to unity, earthly and Divine. There is no unworthiness or inequality within earthly weakness. You need not fear what does not exist or let fear make it so, and you need not remain a stranger to yourself within fear. Embrace earthly chaos and disorder with Love, not fear. Let them lead you from weakness into strength within your Divine Truth.

The Overly Self-Critical Person

The Overly Self-Critical Person is prone to find fault within himself. He has great difficulty distinguishing between the normal weaknesses that all people experience and those that are more unique and significant. Often he is unfair and inhumane toward himself, beating himself up relentlessly for his failures and mistakes. He often has difficulty balancing things out by recognizing what is good about himself and giving himself a pat on the back. This treatment of himself is often a repetition of what he experienced from one or both parents during his childhood years.

Ego's Voice

Your judgments about yourself help to ensure your safety and survival. Embrace them so you will not venture forth to risk danger or destruction. Find the weakness within yourself and do not let it go. Do not rest in your efforts to find your weakness within your thoughts, words, and deeds. Questioning and doubt rooted in fear are your friends. They will lead you to them. Judge yourself harshly so no weakness will be overlooked. You must receive and accept comfort in your weakness. This is where you will remain safe and will survive. Criticism is your oxygen, and you must have it from within as well as from without.

You will survive best within your weakness and must never wander far from it. Do not seek to find strength within, as it does not exist there. Always find what is wrong and not what is right within yourself. The latter are only illusions and distractions. You must not praise yourself, as this will distract you. Do not hear and accept praise from others, as it is false and will misguide you. Rather, invite and allow only criticism from others. Know all of it as dark and real. A reflection and confirmation of your weakness, which you know so well. Weakness is your strength, and you must cling tightly to it. Your weakness shows you who you truly are and must be—a person who is not capable of succeeding.

Look upon yourself as unworthy and undeserving. This will help you to embrace your weakness. Do not seek the joy and happiness that others know, as this is not your destiny. They are for those without weakness. Weakness which you must keep close to you. You cannot overcome your weakness to become worthy or deserving. This would only take away your protection and endanger your survival.

Spirit's Voice

Embrace your weaknesses in Divine Truth and you will move beyond them. Earthly weakness is only a cover for who you truly are. Remove this garment in Love, not fear. Your weakness is a reflection of your humanity. It is not to be feared or attacked. There is no survival to be known by fearing weakness within your thoughts, words, and deeds. This fear is a reflection of your suffering.

Fear is the maker of a harsh judge. Do not let it be the maker of your thoughts, words, or deeds of judgment. Fear within judgment can only lead to unfairness to yourself and others. Love is the maker of a fair judge. Use it to find the earthly and Divine Truth within your being and others. Know your earthly weakness as a place for growth. Do not seek to resist weakness or take comfort in it. These are only reflections of your suffering. Know yourself within Love, not fear.

You have been given important gifts, both earthly and Divine. Seek to recognize and celebrate them in joy. Do not hide them from yourself or others. Accept judgment and recognition from others, which is given in Love. Do not let fear darken them. Raise yourself up in Love so you may serve others well, using your gifts to do great works of service. Do not cower behind fear, which is only a reflection of your suffering. You are meant to know success from your efforts. Do not let fear lead you to see all of the results of your efforts as failure. You can only be deserving of what has been made ready for you— achievement, success, and the Kingdom of Heaven. Do not let fear or illusions of unworthiness let this cup pass from you.

The Clean Freak

The Clean Freak puts forth a lot of time and effort to ensure that she and her surroundings are clean. She feels endangered by dirt, germs, and uncleanliness, which drives her to find it wherever possible in her life. For her, removing dirt, germs or uncleanliness allows her to feel safe. However, this feeling of safety only lasts for a short while, as there is no shortage of places for dirt and germs to make their appearance. Attempts to teach her that they are a normal part of life are likely to fall upon deaf ears as they do not speak deeply enough to her profound sense of vulnerability.

Ego's Voice

You have been led to your cleanliness to ensure your safety and survival. Fear all that is unclean within yourself and others. Seek it in all places, wherever it may lurk. Do not be caught by surprise—find it before it finds you. Stop it before it can begin. You are made strong by cleanliness and weakened by uncleanliness. Vanquish dirt and germs at all times and within all places so they will not weaken or defeat you. Cleanliness is your oxygen, and you must have it.

The unclean are your enemy, and you must fear them. They are the unworthy, the unequal, and the separated. You must not become or remain as one of them. When you are unclean, let fear guide you to the thoughts, words, and deeds that will make you clean. Use them to cleanse all that must be cleansed. They will not fail you.

Avoid all who are unclean, and know them in fear. Keep your distance from them so you will remain safe. They will weaken you with their unworthiness, inequality, and separation. They can only be safe, and become your friends, when they have been made clean. Teach them what they must come to know. Cleanse them with your thoughts, words, and deeds of fear, which will ensure your safety and survival.

Spirit's Voice

Embrace uncleanliness within and around you in Divine Truth. Know uncleanliness as a friend within your earthly being, not as an enemy. A friend with imperfection known to all within the earthly realm. Seek this understanding with your neighbor when called to do so. Thoughts, words, and deeds of Love for yourself and neighbor will make you truly cleansed. Seek, therefore, to cleanse and purify with Love, not fear.

Uncleanliness is a reflection of earthly imperfection. Fear has made it your enemy through illusions of unworthiness, inequality, and separation that illuminate its presence in yourself and your neighbors. Release these illusions while being the Love God Is. You are worthy, equal, and connected within your uncleanliness. Do not create conditions for accepting yourself and others where none exist within the Divine Realm.

Fear is doing more to weaken you than uncleanliness is. Your fear has distanced you from Divine Truth and led you to the suffering you know. This suffering causes you to feel your survival being threatened when uncleanliness appears. Preoccupation with cleanliness has distanced you from your Divine Gifts. You cannot fully know the Gift of Life with its meaning and purpose when distracted by the task of removing uncleanliness. The Gift of Creating Life cannot be known when experiencing thoughts, words, and deeds born out of fear for the purpose of cleansing. The Gift of Eternal Life remains unknown to you when daily life has become a struggle for survival through cleanliness. You cannot know the Gift of God Within when seeking purification with fear rather than Love. Your purification does not lie within the earthly realm, but within the Divine Realm.

The Traumatized Person

The Traumatized Person has been exposed to an event in which he faced the distinct possibility that his life would end. This event often reappears in some way, shape, or form within his thoughts, feelings, behaviors, or bodily experiences. The traumatized person remains connected to the event in order to prevent its reoccurrence and ensure his safety and survival. The event often creates a wall between himself and those who have not encountered a traumatic event, particularly loved ones. It is as though he can never be truly known or understood by those who have not encountered trauma.

Ego's Voice

You have been led you to embrace fear to ensure your safety and survival. Let it be present within all times and all places, be you at work or play, awake or asleep. Let it protect you in your thoughts, behaviors, feelings, and physical experiences, giving you warning signals to prevent another trauma. Do not try to ignore or forget them. Let them connect you to your trauma in order to save you from future trauma. They will not allow the past to become the future. Trauma is your oxygen, and you must have it. You will survive best and remain safe through your connection to it.

Your fear must be greater than the trauma that brought it forth. In fear, you become greater than the trauma. You cannot heal from the trauma, as the future will always occur. You can only shape it with your fear. Fear will prevent you from experiencing future traumas in this way. Thus, it must remain your companion and ally, ensuring that you never again face death's door. Fear will save you from this vulnerability. This is what fear has to offer you, and you must fully embrace it. Abandon your fear, and you risk repetition of trauma.

You can only manage your trauma alone. Those among you without trauma have not lived what you have lived. They do not know what you know and have seen. Ignore their good intensions as they may endanger you with their ignorance. An ignorance that would remove your fear and place you at risk. Your fear is stronger than their thoughts, words, and deeds of ignorance. It will always protect you and keep you safe.

Spirit's Voice

Your connection to trauma is the making of great suffering, not deliverance or salvation. Thoughts, words, and feelings of fear will not lead you to safety, only more suffering, as they cause you to remain a victim of your trauma. They cannot protect you. They only weaken you within the earthly and Divine Realms, due to the distance fear keeps you from Divine Truth and the Divine Gifts. The Love God Is within your being, and within those who surround you, will serve to heal you if you allow it to do so. You cannot know the Gift of Life in trauma. Living in trauma will only lead you to resent this gift, leading a life dominated by your fear of its ending. The meaning and purpose of your life will remain hidden. You cannot know the Gift of Creating Life within thoughts, words, and deeds born of fear of your destruction. The Gift of Eternal Life cannot be known when consumed by fear of your earthly life ending. The Gift of God Within you and others cannot be known within illusions of isolation and separation born of fear.

You need not remain a victim to your trauma. Divine Truth will release you from its grip. You must heal with Love, not fear. When living in fear, your trauma will remain present, and with Love it shall be removed. Fear cannot transcend the earthly realm of your being; only Love can. The Love God Is and You are, cannot be endangered beyond your earthly endangerment. Let be done what has been done, and learn from it what you must. You need not fear the future as you walk into it now with the hand of God.

You must give up your life so that you may have it. When you no longer fear death, you will have life. Love and forgive your enemies so you will no longer fear them and what they have done. Forgive your trauma and stop wishing that it had not occurred, so it will stop. Forgive yourself for any cause of self-blame for your trauma. The Love God Is has no conditions and dwells within you. Walk with it, and it will lead you into the Kingdom of Heaven where fear has no place.

The Order Freak

The Order Freak insists that there must be a great deal of order to what takes place in her life. She invests a lot of time and planning into things going the way they are supposed to go. Rules and doing things in an orderly manner are of paramount importance. She is greatly disturbed when things don't go according to her plan. This violates her need for consistency, predictability, and familiarity while introducing ambiguity into her life. Order removes her sense of vulnerability while disorder serves to enhance it. This need for order can be reflected in many areas of her life. The greater her need for order, the more vulnerable she is feeling.

Ego' Voice

I am the source of your intense need to experience order in the world in which you live, and when you don't experience it, a sense of disorder. Your orderly thoughts, words, deeds, and feelings are rooted in my energy. You and the people who know you well have seen them often. They have been used to maintain order in your life and to impose order upon disorder when it has occurred. Order is your friend as it will keep you distant from your vulnerability. Order is your oxygen and you must have it to ensure your safety and survival.

Order is more important than your relationships with others. Closeness represents a threat to your order as it may call you to acknowledge and respect the order of others which is an invitation to disorder. You can only remain safe within the order you have constructed and known. Let fear assist you in maintaining your distance from others so that your safety and survival will not be compromised by the disorder of others.

Do not listen to those who challenge or raise questions about your ways of knowing order. They do not understand your order and the service it provides to you. Remain deaf to their thoughts and words as they are coming forth from ignorance, a lower quality of order, and even disorder. They do not know how to keep you safe, only you do. Listen to them and you will be endangered.

Spirit's Voice

The illusion of a complete earthly order has led you to seek it within all that you do. An illusion born of fear in which you seek to hide in your thoughts, words, and deeds of order. Each a reflection of suffering manifested in the many times and ways you have imposed unneeded order upon yourself and others while failing to recognize Divine Truth. You have

101

not built a sanctuary with this order, but a prison. A prison in which you must keep distance from the imperfection within yourself and the world. A prison in which you have built a wall between you and others with insistence that your sense of order must prevail within their presence. A prison in which you have been kept from human and Divine Truth. Your prison will be torn down and you will enter the Kingdom of Heaven as you awaken to truth, earthly and Divine.

The order you seek but do not know is Divine Order. It is within this Order that you can reconcile the imperfection and disorder within humanity and the Perfection of Divinity. This reconciliation will help you to answer the call for transformation within yourself, others, and the world, when it is truly necessary. Love and not fear must be the Energy at work in your efforts to know order.

When you have come to know who You are, who God Is, and the Divine Gifts you have been given, you will know the Divine Order available to you and within the world. You will no longer need to suffer within unnecessary insistence for order in the service of your daily and mortal survival. Love rather than fear can be used to embrace the disorder you find within yourself and the world. A Love which teaches there is nothing to fear within disorder and that it can be healed when truly necessary with human and Divine Truth.

CHAPTER 6

Lower Ego Vulnerability Energy

Ego's Voice

You have been led to live without emotion. Emotion is painful because it will let you know what you have done or not done and where you have failed. Without emotion, you need not know fear, guilt, or sadness. You need not know your earthly weaknesses, failures, imperfections, or vulnerabilities. Emotion is a doorway to them, so you must close it off to keep your distance from these enemies. The absence of emotion will make you invulnerable.

When desired seek emotion only for enjoyment. Let it be present within your thoughts, words, and deeds so you can be amused and entertained. Allow emotion to alleviate your boredom so you can know pleasure. Use it as a tool for this purpose. Allow it to be the maker of excitement or interest, where none may exist. Make it a requirement of worthiness when forming your thoughts, words, or deeds. Abandon them when they do not provide the pleasure you desire and seek those which will.

Remain distant from those with whom you work or play. You need not experience emotion in your relationships with them, as it would expose your weakness and vulnerability to them. Both you and they are better off not knowing about your weaknesses. You must not let them know all of who you truly are. The absence of emotion will also make you less obligated to them. When necessary use emotion to experience pleasure in your dealings with others. Be the maker of thoughts, words, or deeds that will bring forth

103

feelings of love, anger, or fear from within yourself and others. Use them as tools for your amusement and to relieve your boredom.

You must be free of emotion in your dealings with those who are closest to you. They will reveal your weaknesses and betray you if you experienced anger, sadness, or fear with them. In their absence you can keep others at a safe distance. Love and fear will bring you closer to them and lead you to need them. It will also make you obligated to them. You are safest and will survive best without these needs. Remain an island unto yourself. When necessary, bring emotion into the company of loved ones. Allow it to arouse, stimulate, and amuse you in the thoughts, words, and deeds of your choosing. Feel love, anger, or fear for the pleasure it can offer you. Emotion is safest when you are able to decide the terms of its expression. This will keep you safe and allow you to survive best.

Emotion will weaken you by forcing you to know yourself. It will lead you to see more of your vulnerability, which must remain hidden. In its absence, you can like yourself more, as you will not have to own or take responsibility for the darker parts of who you are. Allow them to remain strangers to you. Do not allow emotion to concern you with how others see you. In its absence, you can more easily miss, ignore, or dismiss the weaknesses they are calling to your attention. Their thoughts and words can remain meaningless. This will keep you safe and help you to survive.

The work you must do should only be done in pleasure. There is no merit in doing it without pleasure. Seek only what will give you pleasure, and cease doing that which no longer does. You must only use your talents for your amusement. Give to yourself or others only when it will give you pleasure, and do not allow others to ask more of you if it will not give you pleasure. You will survive best through pleasure, not toil.

You must not use the emotions of love or fear to decide what thoughts and beliefs to hold. They can only lead you to what you need to know, rather than what you want to know. What you need to know will lead you to the weakness within your thoughts, words, and deeds which you must avoid seeing. Avoiding emotion will help you to use your thoughts and beliefs without having to own weakness. Learn and use thoughts that will give you pleasure. They will keep you safe and help you to survive well.

You must embrace change as the means to your pleasure. Do not wait for it to occur or be of necessity. Foster it so you can be aroused and stimulated, using change to relieve stillness, boredom, and emptiness. Use the necessary thoughts, words, and deeds that will make it occur. Do not concern yourself with the impact upon others while seeking change, as you are not obligated to them. Only feel the pleasure within these failed obligations if you desire.

The weight of your weakness, imperfection, and vulnerability need not be known within the absence of emotion. All of your failures, losses, and mistakes can be kept at a distance and keep you safe. Sobering thoughts, words, and deeds will not come forth to help you recognize or own your weaknesses. You need not learn from your weaknesses, as there is no emotional weight to accompany them. Enjoy failures if you wish when their impact upon others gives you pleasure.

The emotion you feel must serve your need for pleasure. Do not feel love, hatred, anger, fear, sadness, or guilt for their own sake. Do not allow them to walk you through the doorway to your vulnerability. Use them as a drug when you desire, letting them bring you to bodily experiences of pleasure, and the absence of boredom. You will be safest and survive best when you let yourself experience only the emotion you want to feel, remaining distant from that which does not serve your desires.

You must keep your distance from stressors that come into your life. You need not feel the emotion required to fully recognize them in yourself or the emotion they may trigger in others. You need not recognize how you have been the source of stress for others. You have been made safe from stress and stressors within the absence of your emotion. Stay hidden from your emotion so you will not be weakened and can remain strong, allowing you to survive well. When desired be the stressor for others if that brings you amusement and pleasure.

You have been distanced from conflict by keeping distance from emotion. This distance keeps you from having to recognize the impact of your thoughts, words, and deeds upon others. This prevents you from having to recognize and learn from your weaknesses. Allow your thoughts, words, deeds, and physical symptoms to speak for the anger, fear, or love you must not feel. This will give your emotion a place to go without having to recognize or own it. When desired, force conflict upon others within your thoughts, words, and deeds, so you may enjoy the pleasure it can bring you. You will be safe and survive well when using emotion on your terms.

Spirit's Voice

Your existence is one of great suffering. A suffering in which you are emotionally distant from yourself. A suffering in which feelings of love, fear, anger, or guilt are not available to know yourself and others. A suffering in which you cannot fully own your thoughts, words, and deeds. You cannot truly own the weakness within your earthly being. You cannot fully embrace yourself or understand that you are the Love, Life and Energy God Is. Emotion is but a tool for your earthly amusement. You call upon it for your earthly pleasure, but you cannot know it genuinely. It is but a servant to your earthly needs, which is its only meaning for you. You are often left wandering in pursuit of the next opportunity for pleasure, which has become the essence of your lifeless life.

Your absence of emotion and lack of recognition of your earthly vulnerability have led you to believe many illusions. You have made yourself more worthy, unequal, and separate from others within these illusions. They distance you from Divine Truth and yourself. You have made emotion and weakness unworthy of you, creating an illusion that you are invulnerable to weakness due to your lack of emotion. This illusion serves as a fortress that keeps you apart from and above your neighbors. You look upon emotion as only serving to distort truth, an illusion that has distanced you from yourself and from the ability to witness Divine Truth. These illusions have also greatly distanced you from the Divine Gifts you have received, which are all a reflection of your suffering.

The Love God Is remains at a distance from you. You cannot experience compassion for yourself and your neighbors. Compassion has no place in those who are loveless, guiltless, or fearless. Its absence has left you blind to and removed from your earthly weakness. You do not know the harm you have caused yourself and your neighbors. Being the Love God Is will free you of your emotionless prison. In this freedom, the thoughts, words, and deeds of compassion will come forth to awaken you to yourself and all others.

The Life God Is brings abundant joy and happiness that goes far beyond pleasure and amusement. It is a celebration of the abundance available within Divine Truth, which wells from within rather than from without. Within this celebration, you can give thoughts, words, and deeds of love in service to yourself and others. A service in which your life will have become passionate and meaningful to all you encounter, as well as yourself.

The Energy God Is will allow you to engage in truthful works of thought, word, and deed. An Energy in which emotion will play a role in guiding you to rightful thoughts and actions—it is your friend, not your enemy. Emotions are earthly gifts that bring forth your strengths, not a sign of weakness or merely a means to your amusement.

The Gift of Life with its meaning and purpose can only be known through your earthly emotion. Emotion lets you embrace and celebrate all of the earthly and Divine Gifts you have received. Allow yourself to feel your feelings so you can truly know this Gift. In its absence, your life will remain lifeless. You must laugh in joy and cry in sorrow to know this Gift.

The Gift of Creating Life requires you to feel emotion in order to be a participant in the creation. Let it guide and inform your thoughts, words, and deeds while being the Love, Life, and Energy God Is. Use your earthly emotion to deepen your awareness and acceptance of your humanity. Make friends with emotion and creation so that you will know all that has been made available to you, both earthly and Divine.

The Gift of Eternal Life can be truly known with the Love within your being. Your earthly emotion allows you to embrace both the limited and the limitless—the boundaries of your earthly life, and the unbounded Gift of Eternal Life. It gives you the awareness that you are timeless and endless. You have an unlimited opportunity to enter the Kingdom of Heaven. This Gift has always been available to you, and it always will be. Through your emotion, you will know the ultimate salvation of your eternal life.

The Gift of God Within can be sought and found with your emotion. This earthly gift is the fuel that propels your search and informs the distance you must travel. You cannot be fearless, guiltless, or loveless in your journey home. Know your weakness with your emotion so you may know your strength and that which awaits you, the Kingdom of Heaven.

The Hedonist

The Hedonist has developed an insatiable need for pleasure. She seeks to meet this need at every opportunity and will induce it when necessary. She equates pleasure with happiness, and views its absence as unhappiness. She also feels weakened when she is not experiencing pleasure, an experience she works hard to avoid. Unfortunately, this is the root of many addictions such as alcohol, drugs, food, sex, and gambling.

Ego's Voice

You have been led to seek pleasure to gain distance from your vulnerability. You are strongest when your thoughts, words, deeds, and body are filled with pleasure, so you must pursue all means possible to find it. Allow pleasure to become your addiction. Know your happiness and strength in the pleasure you receive, and know your life as unhappy and lifeless when you lack pleasure. Let pleasure remove all that troubles you. You survive best and are safest when filled with enjoyment. Pleasure is your oxygen, and you must have it.

Ignore those neighbors who would call you away from your pleasure. They can only weaken you and make you lifeless. Ignore any emotion that seeks to interrupt your search for pleasure. Do not listen to fear, guilt, or sadness calling you to work or responsibility. You need not own the past or be obligated to the future. Let pleasure erase your knowledge of your weakness and make you invulnerable. Let it save you from earthly challenges and adversity, shielding you from failure, losses, or mistakes of your making. In pleasure you will be kept strong.

You must use emotion as a tool for finding pleasure. Enjoy fear, anger, guilt, sadness, or love when they can serve your need for pleasure. Foster their appearance within yourself and others to receive their pleasure. Know the worthiness of other people or activities from the physical pleasure they offer you that has been brought from your emotion. Those without pleasure are worthless. Replace those that no longer serve this purpose, as they would weaken you and endanger your daily survival.

Spirit's Voice

You cannot find happiness within pleasure, or by proving that you lack weakness. Finding distance from your weakness through pleasure is only an illusion. Pleasure is the altar upon which you worship, however, and it has become your god—a source of false power and strength revealed by its limited ability to provide happiness. Spending your life moving from one pleasure to another gives you a lifeless, empty, and lonely existence in which you separate yourself from others by avoiding true connection. You have become imprisoned by your drive for pleasure and are within its bondage. You have been made distant from your neighbor by your call to pleasure. You cannot truly know your neighbors, nor they you, when you are consumed by this desire.

Pleasure is the company you must ultimately keep. All are a reflection of your suffering.

Emotion for the purpose of pleasure alone is your enemy. You can learn nothing from it. It has kept you still and stagnant, leading to great suffering. Emotion is to be a tool for growth, not merely pleasure. It serves as a tool with which to find the happiness you are seeking and a means to knowing and accepting your earthly weakness. Allow emotion to call upon you freely so it may serve you. Let it be your friend, dwelling within you when needed. You must truly recognize the absence of happiness to know when it has entered into your life. It will not fail you in your journey to happiness.

The happiness you seek lies within Divine Truth. You will find it within the service you can offer to all while being the Love God Is. It lies within the celebration of God's presence in all of the life that surrounds you. It lies within the Energy you have been given to engage in truthful thoughts, words, and deeds—a happiness in which you are living each of the Divine Gifts in your journey to the Kingdom of Heaven. Illusions of happiness built upon pleasure have no place within this Kingdom.

The Sociopath

The Sociopath has developed a complete disregard for the welfare and rights of others. He can feel no empathy for others or guilt for what he has done to bring harm or pain to others. He often enjoys doing this, as such experiences provide his only opportunities to feel the emotions of anger or fear, which are experienced as pleasurable. If he has a history of being abused, he may seek to become the victimizer so he will no longer be the victim. Victimization of others is a major source of empowerment for him.

Ego's Voice

You have been led to live without emotion so you will know no weakness within yourself. Emotion is your enemy, and you must keep it at great distance. It can only remind you of your weakness. Fear, guilt, and love must remain strangers to you. The absence of your emotion has made you invulnerable and allows you to enjoy the power and strength of your isolation. Isolation from emotion is your oxygen, and you must have it. This is where you are safest and can survive best.

You must trust no one, as trusting others would invite weakness. Trust is an enemy built upon feelings which will lead you to weakness. Emotion can only blind you and lead you into betrayal by others. Remain vigilant for those who may deceive you with manipulation and exploitation. Destroy those who would seek to make you weak. Do not seek to know their feelings, as this would only weaken you. Compassion and connection to others through emotion can only weaken you. You must keep others at a distance so you will not see your weakness within them. Remain separate in your isolation, and you will be kept safe.

Call upon your emotion to create distance from others. Let it create thoughts, words, and deeds of anger and fear for this purpose. Enjoy the anger you have aroused within yourself and the fear you have stirred in others. Enjoy the distance from weakness that comes from within and without using anger and fear wherever and whenever it suits you. They are a tool separating you from the weak, unworthy, and unequal, who are your enemies. These enemies affirm your isolation, invulnerability, and separation from weakness. Remaining separated from them through anger and fear keeps you safest and lets you survive well.

Spirit's Voice

The distance you keep from your emotion is weakness not strength. Living a fearless, guiltless, or loveless existence does not make you invulnerable as you remain an imperfect earthly being. The fear of your emotion has made you weak, not your weaknesses themselves. Your isolation will not fix this weakness. Isolation will only blind you to your weaknesses, Divine Truth, and the Divine Gifts you have been given. The Love, Life, and Energy God Is remains unknown to you within your emotional isolation. You cannot welcome the Divine Truth within yourself and in all that surrounds you when you isolate yourself from others. One cannot truly know a meaningful and purposeful life in the absence of emotion, and one cannot create life with destructive thoughts, words, and deeds. One cannot know eternal life when consumed with earthly survival, or know the God Within if one does not seek God. Your isolation from these Gifts that you have been given is a reflection of your suffering.

You have made enemies of your neighbors and friends through the illusions of separation, unworthiness, and inequality you have created within your isolation. These illusions born of fear are your true enemies, not those who surround you. These enemies lurk within you, not without. The strongest are those who can love everyone despite their own weaknesses and those of their neighbors. Love is a far greater force which resides within you. Strength and invulnerability do not reside in destruction, but in Love, so love your neighbor and yourself.

Your emotion has become a tool for the destruction of others and yourself. This emotion lies hidden within thoughts, words, and deeds of anger and fear, reflections of your weakness and suffering that are leading you further into darkness. You cannot escape these weaknesses through isolation, destruction, and the illusion of invulnerability. God's presence within your being ensures that this cannot occur. Awakening to your Divine Truth will deliver you from the depth of your isolation and destruction. A deliverance into the Kingdom of Heaven that is meant for you and all beings.

The Logician

The Logician seeks to understand and explain all which occurs through logic. She applies logic to all thoughts, behaviors, feelings, and physical experiences. When they do not seem to follow logical principles or reason, she views them as irrational, unreasonable, and senseless. They have no reason to occur, she believes, if logic cannot explain them. Often she discounts emotions and the arts because she views them as illogical. She may hold this mindset because she is gifted with a strong capacity for analytical thought, which mathematical and scientific activities often emphasize. This often reduces or eliminates her respect for the role of intuition in her own life and the world around her.

Ego's Voice

You have been led to rely on logic to find comfort and safety. Logic is the only basis upon which order can exist and your safety can be ensured.

Anything that lies beyond earthly logic can only embody disorder and lead to destruction. Existence can only be found in that which is seen, known, and logical. Know all else as senseless, useless, and weakness. Cling tightly to logic, as this will protect you and keep you safe. Logic is your oxygen, and you must have it.

Within yourself, whatever is worthy must conform to logic. Ignore any of your thoughts, feelings, behaviors, or bodily experiences that are not logical. Evaluate your thoughts, words, and deeds only with logic. The worthiness of tasks must be seen within the logic of their doing. A logic which must be readily apparent. Meet the challenges in your life with logic. The answers can only be found there, nowhere else. Listen with logic to what others are saying in order to judge whether or not it is worthy of respect. When necessary, insist that others learn the logic you know so you will not be endangered by their illogical thoughts, words, and deeds. All of these measures will keep you safe and ensure your survival.

Emotion is the enemy of logic and must be kept at a distance. Do not open the door to your emotion, as it will only weaken you. It will only lead you away from logic, making you vulnerable. It offers an invitation to the unknown, which lies beyond your senses and logic. A distance between the known and unknown which can only weaken you. Emotion can only make the sensible into the senseless. Look upon those showing emotion as weak and less worthy than you. Do not become open to receiving or understanding their feelings, as their weakness may then become yours. You will remain safe and survive well when keeping a distance from emotion, both within and without.

Spirit's Voice

You live within the illusion of an earthly order that can be known, explained, and repaired with earthly logic alone. This understanding of logic does not recognize the limits of earthly thoughts and senses, regardless of the power of your intellect. Human logic can never offer a complete explanation and reparation for all that exists within the earthly realm. Your reliance on logic has distanced you from the reality of Divine Order and the Divine Truth upon which it is built—a reflection of your suffering. What you seek can only be found within Divine Truth. When being the Love, Life, and Energy God Is, all can be known, understood, and healed. This is the making of Divine Order, which will honor your search to know all things.

You have seen logic as a tool with which to defeat the disorder, destruction, and misery you have witnessed within and without. Using logic, you have engaged in a noble yet fruitless effort to confront the seemingly senseless and illogical. The senseless will be made sensible and the illogical made logical within the realm of Divine Order. It is when living within Divine Truth that Divine Order will prevail. Failing to be the Love, Life, and Energy God Is will only lead you to a life of confusion and unhappiness. Earthly logic alone will not change this, as the source of your discontent is beyond the earthly realm and within your ignorance of Divine Order.

The distance you keep from emotion has weakened your connection to Divine Order and the foundation upon which it is built. The tightness with which you cling to earthly logic is a reflection of the fear with which you confront the senseless and illogical. You must release this grip so your emotion can become a tool to knowing your Divine Truth and Divine Order. Do not seek to find them with earthly logic, as they must be found within the mind and heart.

The Loner

The Loner keeps to himself. He interacts with others only when necessary and keeps relationships on a superficial level, spending minimal time with others and sharing little about his life. He is not interested in letting others into his life or becoming part of theirs. Doing so would take him out of his comfort zone. Expressing feelings or tuning into the emotions of others violates his need for comfort. Feelings are best kept at a distance so he can remain alone. An isolation in which he feels safe in keeping himself and others from knowing his needs.

Ego's Voice

You have been led to your loneliness so others can remain at a distance from your needs, which others must not come to know. Your needs shall have no place in your dealings with people. Their knowledge of your needs would serve to weaken you and make you unsafe. This knowledge can only be used against you, not for you. The needy are the weak and vulnerable. Therefore, you must remain an island unto yourself. Loneliness is your oxygen, and you must have it. This is when you are safest and can survive well.

Keep distance from your emotion as it is a doorway to the removal of your loneliness and will allow others to know your neediness and weakness. Emotion can only show you where your weaknesses lie. Absence of emotion keeps you strong and un-needy. Just as you must not call upon emotion within yourself, do not recognize it within others. This would only lead you to weakness. Eliminate all emotion from your thoughts, words, and deeds, which must not stem from emotion. Do not seek honor or praise from others, as this would reveal your neediness and weakness. Remain alone, and you will be kept safe.

Abandon your need for others, and you will remove all weakness. The absence of this need will strengthen you and can remove any fear. Those who are strong need no one else to help them. The weak and helpless are those who need others. You must not be one of them. Leave them to their weakness and helplessness; they are the unequal and unworthy. Keep your distance from them, and you will survive well. The absence of emotion will make this task easier.

Spirit's Voice

The loneliness you seek, not the neediness you want to avoid, is your weakness. Those with earthly needs are not helpless or weak. You cannot disown Divine Truth with your loneliness, and the wall of loneliness you have built cannot isolate you from Divine Truth, only your awareness of it. This Truth is woven into your being. Earthly illusions of separation, unworthiness, and inequality built upon earthly needs cannot unmake this Truth. They are only reflections of your suffering. You will know your strength within connection and unity with others, as all beings reside within Divine Truth. Learn of it within yourself and others. Your suffering born of loneliness will end as you come to know this Truth.

You cannot be made weak and vulnerable by the knowledge of your needs, only by the fear of them. No one can harm you with the knowledge of your needs unless you allow it. Those who would call you to account for your needs with fear or anger are not to be honored. The weak and vulnerable are those who believe they must be without earthly need. Embrace your needs with Love, and allow others to do so as well, and you will be strengthened. There is strength within the need for your neighbor. Need is a force for connection. This connection will allow you to witness the Love God Is that is within and without. You can never be alone when living this Truth, as there is no loneliness within the Kingdom of Heaven.

You seek to make an enemy of your emotion, but it is the means to your truth, both earthly and Divine. Avoiding emotion cannot remove or hide your earthly needs, only your awareness of them. You seek to hide what is revealed within your thoughts, words, and deeds of loneliness. You cannot hide from the Divine Truth that is present within and without. Allow your emotion to serve as a guide to Divine Truth and to all of the strength within your being. Heal yourself with the Love that is within and without.

The Inattentive Person

The Inattentive Person has become oblivious to much of what is going on within and around her. Her attention can only be held by that which is giving her pleasure. She lives in a world of distraction, going from one idea or task to the next before completing anything. When the novelty or enjoyment of an activity has worn off, she is done, even if the task isn't. Boredom comes very easily to her. She does poorly with things requiring planning, organizing, or discipline, as they require effort in the face of boredom. This can apply to her relationships, in which others often experience her as disinterested, insensitive, or reckless, paying little attention to their needs if they do not provide her with excitement and pleasure.

Ego's Voice

You have been led to only those thoughts, words, and deeds that can give you pleasure. Ignore or discard those that do not. Become mindless and emotionless, and do not hear what you do not want to hear from yourself or others. Enjoy all that can bring you enjoyment. Be careless, reckless, or insensitive with your thoughts, words, and deeds when this will give you pleasure. Place no judgment on them, and allow no judgment from without, and you will be free to do all that you want. Hold high regard for yourself, and do not become a witness to your mistakes. Do not learn from your errors, as this will interfere with your pleasure-seeking. You are safest and will survive best within this freedom, which can only be challenged by listening too much to yourself or others. Inattentiveness is your oxygen, and you must have it.

Pay attention to only that which gives you pleasure, and see no value in what does not. Leave what bores you for others to do, and you will not be weakened. Boredom is an enemy that makes you feel weak, empty, and helpless, which you must avoid. Keep distance from your boredom and you will remain strong. Remain separate and above others, who can live within boredom. Do not listen to others who would call you to do boring tasks, as they can only make you weak.

Do not let fear be an obstacle to your search for pleasure. Be fearless, and all will be made available for your excitement and enjoyment. Do not listen to those who seek to awaken fear within you. They can only weaken you with their thoughts, words, and deeds intended to interfere with your pleasure. When desired, expose yourself or others to danger and fear to give you amusement and pleasure. This is its only purpose within your life.

Spirit's Voice

Your deafness to yourself and others is causing you great suffering. It has limited the boundaries of your life to what can give you pleasure, not happiness. You remain hidden from the Gift of Life, as you seek far less than the meaning and purpose it can offer. You have made learning, boredom, and failure into enemies, rejecting opportunities to grow beyond the boundaries of your earthly existence. This is a reflection of your suffering. A failure to listen to yourself and others cannot bring you freedom, only ignorance. It signals an ignorance of the Divine Truth within and surrounding you. You must reach beneath the shallow depth of pleasure to know the greater meaning of your life, a meaning that offers great joy and happiness while freeing you from the search for your next pleasure.

Your deafness has also distanced you from the Gift of Creating Life— the ability to use your own thoughts, words, and deeds to create great wonders that transcend pleasure. Boredom, frustration, and failure call you to something within that is much greater. Do not reject them, as they are friends leading you to a greater meaning and purpose. You have the power to create this meaning and purpose with the earthly gifts you have been given. You have been endowed to create life with these gifts, and with the Divine Truth within your being.

Your inattention has served to fashion illusions of separation, unworthiness, and inequality between yourself and others. Your obligation to others does not cease if you are deaf to their needs. Inattention does not nullify your thoughts, words, and deeds. You must own your moments of insensitivity, recklessness, and carelessness. You are greater than these behaviors, as you are endowed with Divine Truth. The Love God Is within your being knows of your error. Allow it to lead you to own and move beyond your inattention, and to who You truly are.

The Sadist

The Sadist enjoys causing others to experience pain, which can be physical, mental, emotional, or sexual. The perception of pain within other living beings—be they humans, animals, or insects—gives him feelings of pleasure. He may use various forms of torture to experience this pleasure, which is often rooted in the opportunity to release unrecognized and pent up anger. Repetition of this torture also allows him to feel empowered and serves to distance him further and further from his own unresolved experiences as a victim.

Ego's Voice

I am the source of your need to inflict pain upon other living beings. This infliction of pain can take any form that will satisfy your need for the pleasure it brings you. An infliction that will result in any form of distress that is the object of your thoughts, words, and deeds. This victimization ensures that you will never be victimized again. Victimization of others is your oxygen, and you must have it. This is when you feel the pleasure of empowerment and will ensure your safety and survival.

Do not listen to any of your emotions that would have you stop what you must do. Love, fear, guilt, or sadness can only endanger you and return you to the past—a time when you were weak, unlike who you have become.

You are now the victimizer, and the empowered, not the weak and vulnerable victim. Emotion is an enemy, and you must keep it at great distance.

Enjoy and celebrate the victory of your victimization of others. Pleasure is far preferable to the pain you have known. Your pleasure confirms that you are doing what must be done. Pleasure is serving to justify your actions and you must embrace it as your reward for ensuring your safety and survival by victimizing others. Do not stop victimizing others as this will remove your pleasure and place your safety and survival at risk.

Spirit's Voice

You cannot remove your experiences as a victim with the mask of victimizer. A victim you have tried to forget but is within. The victim and the victimizer are the same person. They cannot be made separate by earthly illusions built upon the pain of another. You cannot be made truly strong within the pain you bring to other living beings. This is only weakness and a reflection of your fear and suffering. Pain and fear will only diminish as you come to know Divine Truth.

There is no happiness to be known within pleasure taken in victimizing others, as you are still the victim. You need not be the victimizer to ensure your safety and survival. Your well-being cannot be ensured with pain and fear, which can only make you hollow and lifeless, keeping you vulnerable. You remain vulnerable as you are still the victim. Your emotions of love, guilt, and sadness are the maker of your deliverance, not your betrayal. They are earthly gifts to help guide you to the Love, Life, and Energy God Is and You are. You need not fear them.

You cannot be empowered by the pain you cause others. You can find no empowerment within the illusions of separation, inequality, or unworthiness you have brought to your victims. There is no empowerment in the fear of you that you have brought to them. Pleasure born of others' pain cannot release you from your victimhood. You must heal the victim within yourself to be truly empowered.

You must empower yourself with the Love God Is to liberate yourself from your captor. This is when you are empowered beyond your captor and will no longer fear them. You cannot empower yourself by becoming your captor, as this person also became that way out of fear. Your captor has known your life, and you are only repeating what that person was. The cycle of victimization will be broken by Love, not fear, so those you would have victimized will not become you.

THE TRANSFORMATION

Your Voice

The transformation of yourself and your egoic energy, as well as your ability to speak your voice, has three major contributors: Ego's voice, Spirit's voice, and *Mental Medicine*. Embedded within each of them is the distinction between truth and non-truth, which is the foundation upon which transformation rests. So far you have heard a lot about the first two, and for good reason. You must come to know the voice of Ego and learn of the untruths it has led you to in the name of your survival. Transformation will not occur if you remain ignorant of Ego's voice, no matter how intelligent and well-meaning you are. Intelligence and good intentions are no match for the workings of the unconscious, imbalanced ego. The need for survival, daily and mortal, outweighs one's intellect and intentions. You must also come to know the voice of Spirit and learn about your Divine Truth and the Four Great Gifts with which you have been endowed and empowered. Transformation will not occur if you remain ignorant of Spirit's voice. Truth, human and Divine, is the essential element of transformation. In its absence, transformation cannot occur. The truth must be thought and then spoken in order to be lived.

The third major influence within the transformation process is mental medicine, which we have briefly touched upon. Learning to use mental medicine is no less important than learning to hear the voices of Ego and Spirit, if you wish to undertake the transformation process and speak with your own voice. The use of mental medicine involves progressive awareness of your egoic energy at work as you are living it. You will come to recognize more and more the power, flexibility, and vulnerability of your egoic energy by seeing it reflected within your relationships, achievement, change, and all of the other key areas of life. Your thoughts, feelings, behaviors, and physical experiences within these areas are reflections of this egoic energy. Listening to the voices of Ego and Spirit can point the way to the mental medicine you need to take.

When you are further from the balanced point in your ego power, flexibility, or vulnerability, many of the roles we have described will emerge. When we embody these roles, we have gained great distance from truth, both human and Divine. Transformation can occur when we recognize our distinctive egoic energy. It can be the moment of truth to which we respond. Recognition of any or many of the roles we have been living is the opportunity for awakening which can lead us toward transformation. It can be the moment when our ego stops being a completely unconscious force in our lives. A moment we can begin to stop living the life we were entrapped within and begin living the life we were meant to live.

Mental medicine also involves reality-based thinking that people use to replace the non-reality-based thinking they have been using within the ten key life areas, which again are mirrors of your egoic energy. When using mental medicine, you are making the important distinction between belief and truth, non-reality and reality. As you move closer to egoic balance, truth and reality become more evident, both in the human realm and in the spiritual realm.

Unfortunately, space does not allow us to cover the distinct mental medicine that each particular individual would need to bring about a shift in egoic energy. However, our books *The Ego Unmasked* (Chapters 6–11) and *Ego and Spirituality* (Chapter 7) devote over 500 pages of writing and examples to the discussion of mental medicine. Because egoic energy is diverse, the mental medicine needed to manage yours must be specifically tailored to your egoic energy in order to benefit you within the transformation process. Each of those books is an important complement to *Two Voices* in this way. Each book within the trilogy forms part of a circle leading in an unending path from awakening to transformation to transcendence in which human and Divine Truth can be known.

You may be asking an extremely important question: "Isn't the truth relative?" which rests on the notion that truth is essential to transformation. Without truth, human or Divine, there can be no transformation, only repetition of what has been. This question is also logically connected to references we have made to "your truth", which imply the relativity of truth, particularly within the human realm. Our thorough discussion of mental medicine within our previous books speaks directly to this question. Within the human realm we must each walk our own unique path toward truth which is determined by our egoic energy. A path involving the mental medicine we must each take to move forward into the healthiness that can be recognized in the ten key life areas which is reflective of human truth.

When it comes to "human truth," the discussion of relativity is quite relevant. The egoic mind or ego space is filled with all kinds of knowledge, thoughts, beliefs, attitudes, values, prejudices, and illusions that we have accumulated through our unique personal history comprised of events, relationships, and experiences. We could not possibly be exactly like anyone else, nor they like us. Our human truth is quite unique and relative to who we are. Despite this uniquity, when a person's egoic energy is close to or in balance, they tend to share certain truths. They tend to live within a more consensual, socially-connected, and healthier human reality that rests upon reality-based thoughts shaping behaviors, feelings, physical experiences, and ideas. This healthiness reveals and reflects the power of living within human truth. This tendency shows that many people do share truths even though they are not identical to each other in life experiences.

Just as many unhealthy people living within the roles we have described think the same non-reality-based thinking, so is the case with egoically-balanced people. They tend to think the same kinds of reality-based thoughts when the power, flexibility, and vulnerability of their egoic energy are in balance. Why do we call it human truth? Because they are healthy, and people (including themselves) can see this in the mirror of their life. Healthiness is the reference point of our human truth. The healthier we are, the closer we are to living within human truth. Though this truth is imperfect, healthiness is nonetheless woven into it. We are designed to be healthy and self-healing; we are only removed from healthiness by imbalanced egoic energy leading us away from truth and distancing us from reality, both human and Divine.

For people who venture forth from balance within the power, flexibility, and vulnerability of their egoic energy, the truth becomes quite relative, sometimes to an extreme. They often get lost in their own reality, in a truth founded on beliefs and not truth, either human or Divine. Their beliefs can become quite irrational and faulty, which they cannot recognize due to their ego unconsciousness. A difficulty in recognition which is compounded by the perception of themselves as good, intelligent, and well-meaning persons who are trying to do the right things within their lives. Their primary hope of achieving transformation is "hitting the bottom," where they realize that something very wrong is going on, despite what they had led themselves to believe, and they are at the center of it. This realization can emerge when looking deeply into the mirrors of the ten key life areas, over time if need be. Awakening and awareness can occur within this period of reflection, allowing them to abandon their faulty reality in search of a better one built upon truth, both human and Divine. Many of the roles we have presented are manifestations of the extreme distance from reality that may occur in diverse ways for different people due to the distinctiveness of egoic energy.

Regarding Divine Truth, we believe that it is absolute. We and many others have witnessed the Love, Life, and Energy God Is, both within and without. Divine Truth applies to everyone, at all times, and within all places. There are no boundaries to it, and it cannot be contaminated by human distortions, particularly those offered in the name of religion. We can only create distance from our awareness of it. Divine Truth is your truth and everyone's truth. Rather than defining it, you must awaken to it while walking your own path. God Is Love, Life, Energy, and You. As we said earlier, each were present before humans and human consciousness came into being. We also believe that each of the Great Gifts have been given to all and allow us to live in Oneness and Unity when we have come to know and use them wisely. There is no one who has not been given life, the opportunity to create life, eternal life, and God's presence within their being. We can only remove ourselves from the awareness of these Gifts within the workings of our imbalanced egoic energy.

To transform your egoic energy, you must speak with your voice to your ego. Again, the truth must be thought and then spoken in order to be lived. Your awareness of the untruths your ego has led you to believe, in the name of your survival, will guide your voice in doing so. The human truths you will come to know with the use of mental medicine will also reveal these untruths. Your awakening to Divine Truth and the Four Great Gifts will further inform your voice, relinquishing ego's tight grip upon your survival. As you progressively speak truth to your ego, its grip will relax and your egoic energy will move naturally into a place of balance. That is the incredible power of truth—human and Divine—to bring about healing and healthiness.

Within your human experience, this healing and healthiness will be reflected in reality-based thoughts, behaviors, feelings, and physiology. Each of these components of healing will reveal itself in your relationship with yourself and others, the use of your potential, the growth of your mind, and your healthy management of change, adversity, stressors, and conflict. Finally, you will live genuine happiness and abandon its pursuit in misguided and faulty ways. Human and Divine Truth will have set you free from your darkened egoic energy, and you will be free to live and be who You were meant to be.

You must speak your truth so both you and your ego can hear it, if you wish to build upon what Ego and Spirit have taught you. It is within the speaking of truth, human and Divine, that your egoic energy will be transformed. It cannot resist the power of truth. Speak the truth to it so it will relinquish its efforts to help you survive in unnecessary ways.

You may be asking, "If I were speaking directly to my ego, what would I tell it?" There are several thoughts that ego must "hear" from you, and you must hear them from yourself to move the transformation process forward. These thoughts include:

- Your awareness of its efforts to help you survive within the power, flexibility, and vulnerability of its energy.
- Your awareness of the illusions you constructed that were meant to ensure your survival.

- Your awareness of the suffering that has occurred for you and others for the purpose of your survival.
- Your awareness of the service it was trying to provide you in the name of your survival.
- Your awareness that ego never intended to harm you or bring you into suffering within its efforts to help you survive.
- Your awareness that you cannot seek to disown, dissolve, or defeat your ego.
- Your awareness of the Love contained within your ego's essence is for the purpose of ensuring your survival.
- Your desire to work with your ego as a friend when human experiences genuinely challenge your survival.
- Your accompaniment by Spirit, which has taught you many things about living rather than just surviving.
- Your full awakening to Spirit, which has taught you about Divine Truth, the Great Gifts you have received, and who You are.

A message spoken to your ego would begin something like this:

I know everything about you now and no longer walk in darkness.

I have learned where you have led me and why you have led me there.

I no longer need to suffer in the name of my survival, which was often what you brought me though you did not know or intend to do this.

I realize that I never walked alone, as beyond your accompaniment there always was, is, and will be Spirit.

Your accompaniment is desired, but only when absolutely needed.

The Love within my being wants your presence within it.

I can recognize the Love within your essence and welcome it as my friend....

You must hear your voice, spoken in truth, for you and ego to embark on and move forward along the transformation process. The chapters within the transformation section of this book will reflect the specific messages that must be spoken to ego, dependent on whether one has been living higher or lower ego power, flexibility, or vulnerability. If you are having difficulty tuning into your egoic energy, we recommend that you read Chapter 5 of the *Ego Unmasked*, which describes 125 ego types based on the level of power (size), flexibility (permeability), and vulnerability (fragility) within one's egoic energy.

CHAPTER 7

Higher Ego Power Energy

Your Voice

I have come to know my efforts to exert control over others have been damaging and destructive to both they and I. They were weakened by my blindness to their potential and lack of confidence in them. I can see the resentment I had engendered in them toward both me and themselves. A resentment brought forth within the cowering I had been unknowingly demanding of them. I can see more of their strengths rather than being preoccupied with their weaknesses, which was only intended to empower me. The lessening of my power is allowing me to become closer to them, and they to me. I no longer remind them of others along their life's path who sought to control them for their own needs.

I have stopped trying to think for others and have stopped being fearful of their thoughts. Their thoughts no longer present the challenges I have made them out to be. Challenges intended to lessen my power. I am no longer reckless in speaking my thoughts in ways that are disrespectful of others. I can see as I have awakened, the collisions and wreckage I was leaving behind in my thirst for power. I can see I was not being the Love, Life, and Energy God Is within my thoughts, words, and deeds consumed with power. I can also see how I was removing the Gift of Life from myself and others by the lifelessness my need for power brought to my work and play robbing it of meaning and purpose. Further, I can see how I was denying myself and others the Gift of Creating Life by the boundaries I had placed upon it due

126

to my need for power. I recognize that the many illusions of unworthiness, separation, and inequality I had placed upon others were not based on truth and were only serving to meet my need to feel empowered.

I have come to develop genuine respect for my partner. A person who can never become me in their way of living life and does not need to become me. I can see the need to genuinely listen to what my partner is saying rather than just treating them as voicing idle words to fill space in a conversation. I can see how disrespectful I have been in my deafness to their thoughts, and I have come to understand the importance of their needs within the process of making decisions. I can see the weakness rather than power in striving to often, if not always, get my way. I recognize that my partner has much more to offer me in our relationship than I ever knew, though my needs for power and control had blocked my ability to see these contributions. The lifelessness within our relationship has become clearly evident to me, and I recognize how destructive I had been to it. The word "compromise" now appears within my vocabulary, and I recognize its importance in being connected to them. I now want to create with them rather than for them what can be within our relationship. A creation unavailable when based upon my need for power. A creation greater than what one can do alone.

I now recognize how important their differences from me are to our relationship as well. Differences which are no longer seen through my use of power intended to remove them. These differences can help me to grow as a person, even if I do not fully embrace them or make them a part of me. I want my partner and other loved ones to "breathe" in our relationship by using their own thoughts, words, and deeds. I will no longer suppress and starve them with my needs for power. I want to have intelligent, respectful conflict with them, as I now understand how I can grow from it, rather than avoiding it or dominating them, which is how I have often managed our disagreements in the past. I am willing to close my mouth so I can open my mind.

The recognition of my power has led me to know that I was not being the Love, Life, and Energy I am. Instead of being loved, I was often manifesting anger or fear within myself and my close loved ones. I was making life lifeless and denying my loved ones the Gifts of Life and Creating Life in my intense need to orchestrate life for them. I was limiting my energy by imposing boundaries on it within my power. I can now see how I was weakening my partner's awareness of the Gift of God Within them through my demands for attention and compliance. Now I clearly see all of the illusions that were springing forth from my power. I recognize how I made my partner and other close loved ones appear and feel unworthy, unequal, and separated within my consumption with power, distancing us both from awareness of the Gift of God Within.

I have fallen out of love with myself. Previously, I had seen only what I wanted to see and was blind to the thoughts, words, and deeds I did not want to see. I had felt I could only do right, and no wrong, in my own eyes and those of others. I felt I was above and more important than others, a person whose needs always had to be served. I can now see how others' love for me was tainted by my needs for power. The love from others was distorted by my demands for it, and often offered in fear rather than genuine love. A love that could never be given freely to me due to my needs for power. A love given with a purpose and not to be freely given or received. A love used as a commodity for my empowerment. I can now like and love myself and others in healthy ways, without conditions attached to false empowerment.

The Love I have to offer within being the Love God Is is now freely given to others. I ask nothing in exchange for it. I recognize all people as equally important, with none lesser or greater than myself. I recognize God's presence within each of them, and how we share that endowment. I am my brothers' and sisters' keeper. Their needs are mine, and mine are theirs. We are empowered within our Unity, not within separation. I recognize the Gift of Life each has been given and want to celebrate theirs as well as mine—a celebration that can only be known when all are treated as equal. I now understand that I can only know empowerment through the service I offer to others, not only to myself.

I no longer need to celebrate my abilities and achievements as greater than others. Each has been given their own talents and must be supported in their efforts to use them. These human gifts allow us each to know the Gift of Life and the Gift of Creating Life. These talents were not given for the purpose of comparison or for the defeat of others. I recognize that the record I build with my talents ultimately matters to no one but me. Resting upon my accomplishments is only to live within the past. I should only remember and not revel in what I have accomplished. The only purpose of this record is to let me know how well I have used what has been given to me, not to maintain a sense of superiority. Ultimately, my talents are to be expressed within being the Love, Life, and Energy God Is and I Am.

The link between achievement and self-acceptance as well as the acceptance of others has been broken. I recognize the hollowness of this linkage and how it had obscured my view of the unconditional love that had always been available to me and within me. Achievement cannot make me more worthy, superior, or acceptable to myself or others. These were only notions born within the illusions of unworthiness, inequality, and separation coming forth from my egoic energy. I no longer need to use them to know my talents and achievement.

I now recognize the false enemy I had made of my competitors, and how I had often sought to deny them what I believed only I should have. I now can see the greed within my past thoughts and deeds—a greed born of my need for power. I can now honor others as kindred spirits walking a similar path, and I can celebrate their victories as a culmination of the effort they have placed into using the gifts that all have been given. There can be no true defeat when one communes in Love with others in the use of their earthly gifts.

My mind has been opened so that I can truly know the thinking of others. I no longer readily interpret the expression of their thoughts as an infringement on my power and control. I no longer readily disparage them so I can remain above them. The weakness within this approach has been revealed to me. I now see beyond the illusions which had blinded me to the good ideas, choices, and thinking of others. I no longer see others' good ideas as efforts to control or remove power from me. Rather, I see them as opportunities to grow from what others have learned and know. They are no longer met with suspicion and inappropriate questioning.

I am able to look more closely at the contents of my mind. No longer do I see questioning or changing my thinking as revealing weakness. I now see this ability as a strength built upon the recognition that learning from within or without is an endless process that serves to further empower rather than disempower me. I also recognize how I had disempowered others by controlling their thinking with my thinking and requiring them to close their minds in my presence rather than honor their own thoughts. I can now see the great weakness I had put on display for others, even though I was blind to it myself.

I have learned to encourage the thinking of others even though I may not fully accept or agree with it. Now I welcome the chance to learn about others' knowledge, attitudes, and values so I can know them better. No genuine relationship can exist within the absence of this encouragement. I also seek to encourage and support others with my thinking rather than control them. I no longer attach requirements or consequences to power within our discourse. This is now offered within being the Love, Life, and Energy God Is and I Am.

The changes occurring within me or around me are no longer viewed as a challenge to my power and control. I now understand these changes as being more logical and often inevitable than I had known them. I now understand these developmental, technological, or situational changes have reasons for their occurrence which I had lied to myself about in service to my need for power. My need for power no longer supersedes my ability to see the reasons they occur. I no longer know change as a threat to my power and an enemy to defeat. I no longer possess illusions of egoic control or disorder to support the blindness with which I had known change.

I have learned the difference between controlling change and managing change. Just as I no longer work to prevent necessary change before it can occur, I do not seek to undo change so that things can be what they once were. I do not deny change that has occurred in order to support my need for power. Rather, I value change for its ability to meet a broader range of needs, and not just my own, particularly my need for power. I can now understand the positive transformation often at work in the realm of change which superseded my need to control it. I can see the fear contained within my resistance to change was no match for the Love often at work within the change. I have learned not to take change personally, as it was intended only to lead me into a greater life.

My eyes have been opened to the positive change that has and is occurring within my life, of which I was not the source. Change has often been a friend I have not recognized within the blindness of my power. I can see that change has often given me what I needed rather than what I wanted, allowing me to know a better life, in addition to providing for the needs of others. Change has also been a messenger for the needs of all and not just my own. A messenger which has allowed me to better know the Gift of Life and the Gift of Creating Life. Life and creation are about change, and to fully know them, I must understand this.

The failures, losses, and mistakes which enter into my life are now known as opportunities for growth and not as challenges to my control and signs of weakness. I am now willing to own them rather than looking for other people or circumstances to blame. They are now seen as reflections of my imperfection and not as lessening my power and control. Though I may still not desire them, I accept them as reflections of my humanity rather than engaging in denial with my consumption for power. In this sense, I recognize that I am more empowered than I ever could have been within this denial.

I have also come to recognize how others can help me in responding to adversity. Their thoughts are no longer seen as weaker than my own, so that my need for power could be served and maintained. I also do not see using their strategies for managing adversity as reflecting weakness in myself and lessening my power. Instead, I realize that my brothers and sisters are offering service to me, as I must to them in their time of need. I can now recognize the face of God within their efforts rather than seeing them as attempting to weaken me. They are being the Love, Life, and Energy God Is within these moments. I can therefore honor the Gift of God Within their being by receiving the service they are offering to me.

I no longer attack myself for the failures, losses, or mistakes which have occurred in my life. These attacks stemmed from the illusion that I should have been able to prevent them with my greater power. A power which became open to question upon their occurrence. I now recognize these attacks as born of fear of who I truly am, and I also see that I never needed to fear getting to know myself. I now recognize that I am more empowered by the knowledge of who I truly am—a person with weakness and fault—than by illusions brought forth within my power.

I now understand the difference between genuine happiness and pseudo-happiness—a difference to which I have been blinded in my consumption with power. Their difference has become known upon learning the untruths of egoic power, the human truth within egoic balance, and Divine Truth. I recognize that happiness has no time, place, or cost, as I had believed it did when I viewed it through the prism of power. My happiness comes from within; I no longer seek it without. I now know the pleasure I had gotten from people, places, or objects as the illusion of happiness it was, built upon my need for power. I can now enjoy and celebrate them within the peace and Love of my being. They are no longer a means to an end, but are the end, in which others and I experience mutual happiness simply for the opportunity to be within each other's presence, each a servant to the other.

I now recognize the damage and destruction, large and small, I have brought to others in order to meet my demands for pleasure. Often I made demands by lying, stealing, manipulating, intimidating, or exploiting others. I now recognize that I can never know genuine happiness by treating others in this way. One cannot be the Love, Life, and Energy God Is within this treatment. My happiness cannot come at the expense of another living being, be it an animal, plant, insect, or human. My happiness resides within the recognition, celebration, and use of all the gifts I have received, human and Divine, and within Divine Truth.

I now recognize how often the spaces in my life between times of pleasure were often filled with anger, fear, frustration, and resentment. These emotional experiences came to the surface when boundaries to control over my life or others were being enforced, either by others or life. I experienced these boundaries as threatening and disempowering, but I now recognize them as serving my greater good by allowing me to witness others' use of the Gift of Creating Life. I now see the Love that was being extended to me through them rather than seeing them as attempts to lessen my power, as I had previously known them. I am thankful for the service others were offering to me, even though I was unable to recognize it in my time of need.

The stressors in my life are no longer viewed as threats to my power and control. Whether they involve health, finances, family, relationships, or work, I know they are not intended to weaken or disempower me. As I have removed my faulty interpretation of them, I have come to recognize them as inevitable occurrences within the human condition. They do not seek to defeat me, but to call upon my talents and resources, both human and Divine. I no longer seek to defeat or destroy them in order to remove their threat to my power.

I recognize how difficult it was for others to be near me when I sought to defeat stressors. The tension and stress I had created for others with my words, feelings, and behaviors. I often directed my anger at them in a misguided effort to deal with the source of my stress. Some of which I felt falsely entitled to express. I can now see how weak I really was. I thank them for standing by me until I awakened. For those who could not, I understand their leaving and hold myself responsible, not them, for this occurrence. I wish them well and hope they can live in peace in the company of others, which they truly deserve.

The true source of my stress has been me. My need for power has enlarged many of the stressors I have encountered. I now recognize that I have been my greatest opponent and enemy, though this has changed as I have awakened to human truth and Divine Truth. Awakening to each of the Divine Gifts has taught me that I no longer have to fight for my daily survival and empowerment. My daily and eternal survival has already been assured.

The conflicts I experience with others now occur in a far different light than the darkness I had known within my hunger for power. A darkness often making for frequent, intensive, and unnecessary conflict. A darkness in which there could only be one victor, me. A darkness in which I aimed to thoroughly vanquish my opponents so as to remove them from future efforts to defeat me. It was within this darkness that I often demanded that others think my thoughts, use my words, and do my deeds in order to seal the victory. This darkness has been removed by the light of human and Divine Truth. A light that has shown me that conflict is the means to growth within myself.

I now recognize that the one victor who must emerge from the conflict is not myself or my opponent, but the relationship. So often I have won the battle but lost the war, which was the relationship. I have not been the Love, Life, and Energy God Is and I Am within these encounters. I was not being of service to others even if my thoughts, words, and deeds were superior to those of my partner, children, or others. I had gotten lost within the merits of my position while failing to see the process unfolding before me. A process often containing contempt, degradation, sarcasm, and humiliation for those who opposed me. I was often blind to it and if I did see it, I did not care. Winning was the only thing that mattered. I now see that as I was winning, I was only losing.

I want to apologize to all those I have mistreated in serving my need for power. I now seek to honor and respect them within our differences whenever and wherever they may occur. I will endeavor to truly listen to them before formulating my response to their positions. I can agree to disagree with them, as I recognize that we often come from two different earthly worlds that have made each of us who we are within the human realm. I no longer seek their defeat, as I recognize the disempowerment this would bring to me.

CHAPTER 8

Lower Ego Power Energy

Your Voice

I have stopped being the follower I so desperately needed to be—someone who stood in the background waiting for others to provide guidance. I have come to know there is much more to me than I ever knew or would let others know. I know that I cannot live by surviving within the shadow of others. I now recognize that neglecting my thoughts, words, and deeds has prevented me from being of service to others and myself. I will no longer hide from others in the name of protecting myself, as there is no real protection to be known within the shadows—only loneliness, emptiness, and isolation.

I will no longer hide my successes from myself or others, seeing them as fortuitous accidents or attributing them to the talents or benevolence of others. Illusions of separation, unworthiness, or inequality no longer distance me from them. Rather, I can now celebrate my successes as reflections of the human and Divine Gifts I have been given. I see them as something I was intended to experience, not as accidents. I understand that I am responsible for them, and I take ownership for their occurrence.

I will no longer fear failure and its opportunity to expose me and others to any of my weaknesses. My weaknesses, wherever they may lie, are no longer excuses for avoiding failure. As I have awakened, I have come to realize that failure to try is the real failure. I now have the courage to fail, wherever it may find me and rise up from failure, rather than remaining on the ground. I no longer listen to those who would attack me for my failure.

They do not have my interests at heart as I had so often thought. They were only serving their own interests, which often centered on keeping me exactly where I was. I now only listen to those who support me, as they see in me the gifts that I am coming to know. I also realize that many have walked a similar path of failure on the path to success. The only real difference between them and me is that I am just beginning to walk it.

I am no longer a passive and submissive participant in my relationships with those who are closest to me. My partner will no longer define me in my thoughts, words, and deeds. I no longer seek refuge in others, and must stand on my own. There is no safety or survival to be known in becoming them, only a hollow life. I realize how absent I have been within my relationships. An absence which has been unfair to myself and my partner and loved ones. This absence is ending as I learn how important I am to these relationships. Communication is now a two-way street as I must be listened to as well as listen. My thoughts and words at times may not be as good as those of my partner, but they are no less worthy of honor and respect, if not agreement. Expression is what must be present, not agreement.

I now insist upon compromise when differences cannot be completely resolved—compromise that respectfully honors my needs as well as those of my partner. Illusions of separation, unworthiness, and inequality no longer fill my mind to prevent me from receiving what I deserve within relationships. I am worthy of genuine compassion from my partner and other loved ones, not pity within my time of need. I am not someone to feel sorry for, but sorry **with**, *when I need to be lifted from darkness and bring a smile to my face. I am someone worthy of receiving the Love, Life, and Energy God Is from others, which I seek to offer others in turn. I now seek to create life through communion with my partner, rather than waiting for my partner to create it for me. The Gift of Creating Life was given so I can use my thoughts, words, and deeds to create the life I want and the relationship I want. I have neglected this Gift for so long in fear that they would not be adequate. However, I have abandoned the fear of using the wrong thoughts, words, or deeds. When being the Love, Life, and Energy God Is, the creation of life can only be positive and transformative, I understand.*

I am no longer a hostage to my relationship with my partner. Someone chained to the relationship within the fear of its ending. I no longer tolerate abuse, manipulation, exploitation, or humiliation as the price of remaining in the relationship and receiving my partner's protection. I can offer to myself what my partner has been unwilling or unable to offer me. I am giving myself the empowerment of human truth and Divine Truth. An empowerment in which I am free to breathe and become the best possible version of myself.

I am now able to like and love myself as I am. I have learned to be fair to myself and can give to myself, no longer viewing this as unhealthy selfishness. I do not need to perform or achieve things to like and love myself. I recognize that there can be no conditions or criteria to be met when one knows the Love God Is and I Am. There can be no future time for its occurrence as this Love can only be now. It has no time, place, person, amount, or burden. All of these requirements were built on the illusions of separation, unworthiness, and inequality I have known in the name of my daily and mortal survival. I now know that the Love God Is within me is pure and cannot be contaminated with any of these conditions.

I am now able to offer love to others freely. Illusions of unworthiness, inequality, or separation no longer prevent me from its expression. I no longer question its merit or fear that others will reject it. Those who are ready can receive it, and those who are not can do so when they are ready. There are no requirements for this Love, nor any weight or burden to my loving thoughts, words, or deeds, as I do not seek its recompense. I give my good works freely by being the Love, Life, and Energy God Is.

I welcome the love of others as an opportunity to experience the Love God Is from them, of which I am worthy. I do not seek their approval or acceptance as a substitute for the absence of my own as this absence no longer exists. Because I feel the Love that has always been given to me from within, I no longer wait for love from my loved ones. I can give to myself in loving ways even when others have failed me in being the Love God Is, and I can continue loving them, which is being the Love God Is and I Am.

My talents are becoming better known to me. They are no longer being hidden from me, by myself, or by others. I no longer see their use as an infringement upon what others may want or need. I now understand that the process of working to use one's talents is open to everyone, even if we may not know the same result. I also know that my successes do not truly stand in their way. Everyone must know the path of success and failure or defeat. A journey when taken which can lead us to what is greater within ourselves. That is the true purpose of competition and achievement. Records and trophies are tributes to this journey and beyond this are meaningless.

I am no longer fearful of any of my weaknesses or limitations. I no longer use them as excuses to prevent me from using my talents. They no longer shield me from the arena of competition in the name of my safety and survival. I now accept them as reflections of the imperfection of my humanity. I work to heal them as needed, no longer seeking to hide them. They have also led me to know the Perfection of my Divinity—a Perfection known within being the Love, Life, and Energy God Is and I Am.

There is no longer a need for making faulty comparisons or setting unfair standards for myself. A faultiness which failed to recognize the different nature of my abilities with those of my neighbor, and the different contexts we have walked through, which have helped or hindered our progress and growth in different ways. The only frame of reference that matters to me is myself. I have come to know in truth who I Am. I know where I was, where I am, and how far I must go in using my talents. I can only compare myself to myself to truly know the journey I must make. It is not for others to tell me who I can be or not be, where I can go or not go, or what I must become or not become. Even if these are well intended, they can only lead to living the achievement of someone else's vision of me. I am to be the maker of this vision and the climber of my own mountains.

I am now the maker of my own thoughts, words, and deeds. No longer do I look to others for their making. Illusions of separation, unworthiness, and inequality, no longer prevent me from their construction. The Gift of Creating Life is allowing me to be the creator and not only the created. I have been given this Gift so that I can do wondrous things with my mind while being the Love, Life, and Energy God Is. A mind I had often neglected and allowed ownership to others due to my illusions of inferiority and weakness.

I am now able to trust my mind in ways I had not been able or willing to do before. The failings which may come forth from my mind no longer frighten me and lead me into abandonment of my thoughts or abdication of my thinking. I understand that my human imperfection may lead to errors, and I no longer seek to avoid these errors within the faulty name of my safety and survival. I know that I was given the Gift of Life in order to be the thinker of my thoughts and the owner of my life so I can know its meaning and purpose.

The ownership of my mind has allowed me to decide what must be added, changed, or removed from it. I no longer look to others to determine my thinking. Respect for others or their good intentions are no longer sufficient reasons for unquestioned acceptance of what they would have me think or not think. I remain willing to accept their counsel, but no I longer do so blindly. I also recognize that others are fallible, and that this responsibility cannot be given to others or imposed upon me in the ignorance of this truth. Their thinking and thoughts are also recognized as often working better for them because of who they are within the confines of their life. There is no longer any requirement to conform my thoughts to theirs or sense of dishonoring them if their thoughts are not chosen. Those who would seek to impose their thinking on my own are now seen as disrespecting and dishonoring me. I no longer see them as strong, but as weak within their failure to honor me while being the Love God Is.

I no longer feel overwhelmed by or fear any of the change which comes into my life. The person who often hid from changes in health, finances, work, or relationships no longer exists. I no longer seek to ignore, deny, or wait for others to manage change on my behalf. Change is not seen as problematic, larger than me, an opportunity to defeat me, or as a threat to my safety or survival. Rather, I am recognizing it as an inevitable part of my life that cannot remain still in the name of my safety and survival. I am now prepared to meet change and embrace it with the empowerment of human truth and Divine Truth.

I walk with change as my friend, not as my enemy. I now recognize that the enemy it had represented to me existed within myself and in my unwillingness to manage change—an unwillingness built on illusions of separation, unworthiness, and inequality I had been holding of myself. I have relinquished all requirements that change be consistent, predictable, and familiar, as such requirements impose boundaries upon change, life, and energy. Such boundaries could only be built on illusions of egoic control and order. The empowerment of human and Divine Truth has released me from the need to place boundaries on what may enter or leave my life.

I now meet change with understanding, not ignorance. My empowerment has allowed me to feel entitled to manage it, which I could not have experienced within the illusions of separation, unworthiness, and inequality. I now recognize what change can offer me, and what I can offer in turn. Change calls upon me to use my resources, both human and Divine, which I had so often hidden from myself and others. Change provides a call for movement and transformation in my life, which I have learned is ultimately good when I meet it with human and Divine Truth. When it is painful to me, change leads me to examine how I am not fully living my human and Divine Truth. Change is woven into the fabric of life and my

138

life. Without it, there can be no life, only existence. Change is an inevitable reflection of the Love, Life, and Energy God Is.

I no longer meet adversity with avoidance and paralysis, which was rooted in my fear of being consumed by whatever unfortunate event may enter into my life. These events be they failures, losses, or mistakes are no longer known as the enemies I once knew them as. I no longer see them as threats to my safety and survival. Rather, I now know them as friends, simply reflecting the imperfection of my humanity—an imperfection that resides in all human beings and which in its own way connects us to each other. I will no longer run from adversities or look to others to shield me from them. They are opportunities to grow and I will know them in this light.

I have learned to view adversity from a far different perspective. No longer do I see its making as only within the realm of my weakness and imperfection. Its making is now seen as more complex and at times beyond the reach of my weakness. This insight is not the making of blame as that would serve no purpose, but understanding. In this regard, I am becoming more fair to myself. I also see how I had been magnifying the size and frequency of problems through the lens of my helplessness. A helplessness born of illusions of separation, unworthiness, and inequality. Illusions that were serving to disconnect me from human and Divine Truth. Illusions that often had me believing that life was out to get me and that I deserved less rather than more from life. These illusions have been removed and with that I am empowered by truth, human and Divine, to manage all that may confront me from within or without.

I no longer require the assistance of others to manage the problems that have been brought to my door. Rather, I now call upon the human and Divine Gifts I have been given to meet these challenges. Human and Divine Truth has empowered me to answer the call of failure, loss, or mistakes which may visit me. It is within these Gifts and Truths that no failure, loss, or mistake is too great to be managed while being the Love, Life, and Energy God Is and I Am. This is also offered to my neighbor as I am always available to them in their time of need. We are each our brothers' and sisters' keeper and must offer service within the time of need.

I have relinquished the sadness and depression that has so often emotionally colored my life. Emotions entrenched by the helplessness, hopelessness, and pessimism that had so often dominated my thoughts and led to lacking a sense of control within my life. I now see how often such thoughts were being used to protect me and to ensure my safety and survival. A means to empower myself within my disempowerment. An empowerment built upon the illusion that if I remained distant from myself and others in my thoughts, words, and deeds I would be fortified. I now realize that I had not built a fortress, but a prison. A prison in which all of my thoughts, words, and deeds were being chained to prevent their free expression, ultimately keeping me within my sadness and depression.

My sadness and depression has so often kept me at a distance from others in the hopes of remaining safe from them and their judgments of me. So often I have filled in this distance with faulty beliefs of who they were and what they thought of me. Beliefs built upon illusions of unworthiness, inequality, and separation that I carried within and attached to them. These illusions prevented me from becoming aware of the Love, Life, and Energy God Is within all of us. I no longer harbor these illusions, as human and Divine Truth have taught me they are false. I no longer have any need to fear others, too, as I know who they truly are. They are to be my servants, and I theirs, as we celebrate all of the gifts we have been given and embody the Love, Life, and Energy God Is.

I have ventured forth on the path to happiness—a path I have so long avoided due to its invitation to the unknown. Fear has so often prevented me from walking this path. So often, I have retreated into the comfort of depression, which rested upon the consistency, familiarity, and predictability of the known, rather than the unknown. It may have felt ugly, but it met my needs for safety, protection, and survival, which I now know as an illusion. My journey is now fueled by human and Divine Truth, which have empowered me to be the Love, Life, and Energy God Is and I Am. Love is a far more powerful force than fear, and I have learned that it will answer and defeat any fear I may know in my journey to genuine happiness. It is the key that has unlocked the door to my prison and freed me to undertake the journey. Fear is no match for Love's presence and is only empowered by Love's absence.

I now see the true size of the stressors that enter my life. They are no longer magnified by an absent sense of power within my being. An absence which often led me to know them as larger than any power to manage them I possessed. Thus, they are no longer the predators I had known them to be, waiting around every corner of life. They do not seek my defeat or destruction, as I had believed. I have always been empowered to manage them, though I did not know it, and this empowerment is growing within my connection to human and Divine Truth.

I now answer the call of stressors with the thoughts and behaviors that are required. Thoughts and behaviors containing empowerment rather than weakness. My body no longer needs to respond to stressors alone with various forms of stress symptoms. I now recognize that the stress I felt was often far greater than the stressor that brought it forth. I now feel stimulation from many of the former stressors that had consumed me, as my perceived capacity to manage them has grown. No longer do I see them as an enemy or wish them to be absent from my life. I now recognize that this would not be possible, as challenges and changes are part of the essence of human life. Within their absence there would not be life, but lifelessness.

I no longer seek others to manage what I can manage myself. Asking others to do what I could have done for myself so often served as an affirmation of my powerlessness and helplessness which I was unable to recognize. I can see now how asking others to do what I could do for myself served to entrench each of them. When looking back on particular times when my neighbors refused to help me, I realize this was often an act of kindness, not rejection. They were encouraging and believing in me when I was unable to do so for myself. They were giving me not what I wanted, but what I needed, and being the Love God Is.

I now welcome the opportunity to participate in healthy conflict with others. These conflicts no longer represent opportunities for humiliation or defeat within the expression of my own thoughts and choices, but opportunities for growth. No longer do I readily conclude that my thoughts and choices are weaker because they came from within me. No longer do I question my right to express them in deference to others. No longer do I readily conclude that the thoughts and choices of others must be better because they are not mine. The illusions of separation, unworthiness, and inequality no longer exist to support these beliefs. All human beings have been given the gift of a human mind that is meant for them to use and not ignore. Conflict is but an opportunity to use this gift in service to myself and neighbors.

I now recognize that conflict represents a chance for growth, not destruction. It presents an opportunity for each of us to learn from others, when used wisely. It also provides an opportunity for each of us to be the Love, Life, and Energy God Is by seeking to serve each other rather than just ourselves. I now recognize those who seek to do the latter, as they reveal themselves in the various ways they seek to dishonor, disrespect, or defeat my ideas and choices. Ways that may involve insults and intimidation. I now recognize the weakness rather than strength within their tone and efforts. I need not engage them, as nothing can truly be gained within conflict under these conditions.

I now recognize I can only be a winner if I have partaken in healthy conflict. Winning involves learning more than I knew before the conflict which can be used to serve me. Winning which involves sharing what I know which can be of service to others. Winning which involves the experience of mutual respect which occurs despite the nature of our differences. My neighbor does not need to become more like me, nor I like them, in order to know this respect. We are connected within our human differences by being the Love, Life, and Energy God Is which, is our ultimate likeness. We do not need to become this within the human realm as our Unity and Oneness already is.

CHAPTER 9

Lower Ego Flexibility Energy

Your Voice

I've been opening my mind to myself and others as I work and play with them. No longer do I instantly find deficiency in the differences of others from myself. I am able to respect these differences as opportunities to learn what they may be able to teach me and not reject them. So often, I had rejected these differences regardless of their merits. I now honor all whom I encounter, even though I may not agree with their ideas or ways of doing things. I now recognize the diversity of Love, Life, and Energy God Is reflected within each of my neighbors—an awareness to which I had so often been blind.

I now realize that I am not the owner of the truth, earthly or Divine. An ownership I had so often attempted to force upon others. I had so often demanded that others know and think my thoughts while abandoning their own, an approach that was utterly disrespectful despite my good intentions of helping them with my knowledge. I had been so lost within my convictions that I did not see the truth others may have known. My conviction often prevented me from questioning my thoughts and searching for better ones. I now seek to live the truth, not own it, wherever I may find it.

I now see my neighbors in a different light as well. A light in which I recognize that their human truths have been fashioned by the times, places, and events of their life. Each unlike anyone else who has ever lived. Their minds cannot be like mine any more than their bodies can be like mine.

143

Though we may be of different minds and bodies, we all have been given the Divine Truth and the Divine Gifts. I now recognize that this is where our Oneness and Unity truly resides. There is nothing within the human realm which can take its place.

I no longer ask my partner or other loved ones to think my thoughts in order to experience closeness to them within our relationship. They no longer have to think like me so we can be on the same page—my page. I realize how harmful and destructive to our relationship, and to them, I had been when placing this requirement on them. I was asking them to be less like themselves and more like me—a false premise for connection and unity. I can see the pain I had caused them by asking them to give up parts of themself to keep peace and me in the illusion of peace. I had made our relationship not full, but hollow by asking them to lose themselves within it.

I no longer fear any of their differences and will treat them with respect. Their thoughts and feelings are important ingredients to the growth of ourselves and our relationship, I now understand. These ingredients stimulate communication, compromise, compassion, and creation within the relationship. Our relationship is no longer stale and static from my domination of the ideas expressed within it, which only served to stunt the relationship. Rather, our relationship has become dynamic because I have learned to welcome the energy that has always been waiting to be expressed. We have been made young, vibrant, and excited by the opportunities to grow from each other. This growth has no end, I have realized, as there are no limits to the Love, Life, and Energy God Is and We Are.

I now feel closer to my partner and other loved ones than was ever possible within the realm of my closed, inflexible mind. I had been attempting to fashion this closeness with my version of the truth, upon which I believed we could both stand. This truth held many illusions, particularly the illusion of inequality. Though my intentions may have been good, our closeness was only an illusion that existed in the service of my needs. I have been awakened to a greater truth, Divine Truth, and the Divine Gifts. This awakening has given me a sense of Oneness and Unity with others and a closeness of the mind and heart which could never be known alone within the human realm.

The value I hold of myself is no longer built upon ownership of the truth within my thoughts. So often I had thought of myself as superior due to my supposed ownership of the truth. An ownership in which I had placed myself above others and saw them as beneath me. An ownership in which I had believed my ideas, beliefs, values, and knowledge were above those of others. An ownership which I now recognize was only a self-serving illusion. The more I had been striving to own human truth, the more I was disconnecting myself from Divine Truth. The more I sought to raise myself up, the more I was lowering myself down. I was preventing myself from being the Love, Life, and Energy God Is and I Am.

I now welcome and value what others bring to me with their distinct thoughts. No longer do I view it through the lens of my superiority with which to esteem myself more and others less. I realize no higher or healthy self-esteem can rest upon this foundation, as I cannot truly raise myself up by lowering others. All must be raised or none will be. We are all truly connected to each other when all is seen and one has been awakened to the Divine Truth within all beings.

I no longer feel weakened by the discovery of limitations within my thoughts and thinking. These limitations no longer pose the threat to my superiority that I had known them to be. Limitations which I had worked so hard not to see or for others not to see. I now see how acknowledging them builds the strength of my character and opens me up to a greater human truth than I have known. I am now able to fully know and accept myself as I truly am, which is the foundation of self-esteem and truly loving myself.

My mind is more open to what I or others can achieve. I no longer impose faulty notions of what should or should not be achieved upon my work or the work of others. These notions were often built on my own definitions of importance, which I applied to everyone. I had so often disregarded and disrespected my own achievements or those of others with this faulty definition. I now recognize that we must each decide what is important to us, and how we can best use our talents to accomplish it. All must be supported wherever their interests and talents may lie while being the Love, Life, and Energy God Is.

I also no longer employ faulty criteria by which to judge the success of my efforts or those of others. I have so often made harsh, unfair judgments about how others or I were doing in our journey to success. So often I have missed or overlooked factors that impacted our effort or success. I now see more of the process of achievement as well as the outcome, which has taught me to learn more about myself and others before passing judgment.

I am able to listen more to those who can offer a well-informed, realistic appraisal of my abilities, potential, and performance as well. I no longer listen to no one, those who tell me what I want to hear, or those who will affirm what I already know. Those who would tell me new or different things about my potential and performance are no longer instantly rejected. I now welcome new information about my abilities, weighing these insights and observations with the respect they deserve. I can now hear what I have not wanted to hear, be it positive or negative, which is helping me to more truly know my abilities and performance. I thank others who offer this feedback, be they teachers, coaches, supervisors, friends, or my partner.

I have abandoned the illusion of possessing an absolute human truth that everyone should know. I realize others are living their truth based on the path they have walked in this earthly life—a path unlike any other. I now respect their path where once I dishonored it. A dishonor built upon all of the differences I saw in their path as being deficient. I now know their differences from me are not deficiencies, though I had seen them as such through the illusions of unworthiness, separation, inequality, and sensing all energy. These illusions have disappeared as I have come to recognize the Unity and Oneness of being the Love, Life, and Energy God Is.

My mind has been opened. For too long I had listened only to myself or those who thought like me. For too long I had known myself as a finished product, having arrived at the fountain of truth. For too long I had nowhere to go but convert others to my truth. I recognize the fallacy in each of these ideas, and I have now become a student of myself and of life—a never-ending journey within the earthly realm, whose end I no longer seek. This journey can only end when one fully knows Divine Truth and enters the Kingdom of Heaven.

The opening of my mind has allowed me to healthfully modify my thoughts and beliefs, which has allowed me to form a tighter connection to the broader human reality that surrounds me. Through this connection, I have learned how different ideas, beliefs, values, and knowledge have often served others well. I have also come to recognize how the Love, Life, and Energy God Is was making its presence known within all of the different beliefs and ideas that others hold just as it has done within my difference from others. Difference within the mind of others is no longer the weakness or enemy I had made it out to be; it poses no threat to my safety. Changing my own mind in response to these differences no longer signifies weakness to me, either. They are no longer the threat to my safety and survival my closed mind had made them out to be. I welcome the differences of my brothers and sisters, knowing that ultimately we are the same within Divine Truth.

I am now able to think about the changes in my life in a different light, particularly the larger, rapid, or unexpected ones. They are no longer being forced into the compartment of a closed, inflexible mind. A mind which often insisted on understanding any change through the lens of the ultimate truth I believed I already held—and managing it by ignoring, resisting, or rejecting it—this is no longer acceptable to me. I had so often tried to turn back the clock or kept time still by using only what was familiar to me. An attempt that was only an illusion as I now recognize that time and change were marching on with or without me.

I have acquired new allies in my efforts to work with and manage change. These allies include new, different, or better ideas which allow me to know the change in the light that it truly exists, rather than the dim light or darkness of dated thinking. I welcome those neighbors whom I have known as different to offer their contributions to the depth with which I can think about significant change, understanding that they can offer valuable rather than deficient viewpoints based on their life experience. This awareness stems from the recognition of the Love, Life, and Energy God Is within all. I no longer believe that I, or those just like me, are the only ones capable of managing change.

The opening of my mind has allowed me to strike a greater balance between tradition and progress within myself and the world. I remain connected to many of my existing thoughts that have served me and others well, while opening up to the different or better ones in order to live fully in the present. I recognize the inevitability of change, as its source is energy—a diverse, unlimited energy that no human thought can contain. This positive, transformative energy allows for growth through the change it is creating. Change is now my friend, as it has always been, though I did not know this. I no longer need to shield myself from it with my thoughts.

I am now able to confront the problems in my life with a broader range of understanding and solutions. So often I had used black-and-white thinking to confront many of the shades of gray upon which human reality and imperfection is built. I no longer insist on managing adversity only in familiar ways, an approach which often blinded me and kept hidden what was deeper and beneath the surface. This often kept me from recognizing the true nature of the problem because I was trying to solve the one I expected to see. I now solve the problem that truly exists, not the one I want to exist. I am no longer fearful of finding more than I want to find or knowing more than I want to know.

My door has become open to all who can help me along my journey. I call upon their different or unfamiliar thinking to assist me. I am open to their service, and offer mine to them, while we are both embodying the Love, Life, and Energy God Is. Genuinely calling upon this service when it can be of help to me reveals no weakness. I now realize that we are all called to be of service to each other as we make our way along our path. There can be no wrong person to listen to or from whom to receive guidance when being the Love, Life, and Energy God Is.

Similarly, I can now stop listening to myself and hear others better who need to be heard within my time of need. I realize I do not know everything that can be known within the human realm, and I no longer fear the acknowledgement of this human truth. This acknowledgement reflects strength, not weakness, as I had previously believed. This truth need not be feared when living within the realm of Divine Truth. No human failure, loss, or mistake can remain unhealed when embracing Divine Truth and the Divine Gifts I have been given. Both human and Divine Truth have set me free from fearing the weakness of my humanity.

I have come to know the connection between my feelings of anger, fear, or depression and the non-reality-based thoughts I formed to understand myself, others, and events in the world. My often narrow version of reality led to frustration and resentment when I could not remake the actual reality into the idealistic image of what I thought it should be—an image of black-and-white truth, of which only I could be the creator.

For so long, I had struck out at those who did not comply with my image of reality. I had either struck at them with my thoughts, words, or deeds fueled by my seething anger or fear, or I had silently struck at them by quietly expressing my emotions in more subtle thoughts, words, or deeds. In either case, I did not realize what the emotion was truly telling me. I had so often interpreted it, when I could see it, as an affirmation of my truth; as fuel to be used in bringing others to the truth I knew. I now see that it was telling me how far I was from the truth. The greater my anger, fear, or sadness, the greater my distance from the truth, both human and Divine. My thoughts had gotten lost in the land of faulty beliefs. Beliefs built upon all of the illusions I had embraced in the name of my safety and survival.

I have come to know that the only emotion that can guide me to the truth is Love—an emotion that enables me to see things more broadly. Love makes my thoughts more inclusive than exclusive. It recognizes the breadth of life and energy that surrounds me, which I had been denying myself. This life and energy has always been within my being, and I will no longer hide it from myself or others with faulty notions. Notions which require people to assume my likeness within the human realm. I now realize we all share the same likeness within the Oneness and Unity of the Divine Realm.

I no longer manage the stressors that enter my life with thoughts of ignorance. Thoughts in which I knew myself as knowing the only right ways to manage them. Thoughts in which I believed I was immune and beyond the reach of any stressor. Thoughts in which I saw myself as "larger" than any stressors that came my way. I can now see how these thoughts were hiding the stress I was actually experiencing. Stress was revealing itself within my thoughts, behaviors, feelings, and physical symptoms, and I could not truly keep it from my door with ignorance. Unrecognized stress does not become nonexistent, I have learned.

I no longer believe that succumbing to stressors and stress reflects weakness. The true weakness lay within my failure to acknowledge them when necessary. I had been denying my human imperfection rather than working with it, just as I had been denying the Perfection of my Divinity, which could have helped me to meet the challenges before me. Through each of these denials, I made myself weaker than any of the stressors I faced. I have learned that truth, human and Divine, will deliver me within my time of need. Through this truth, Love rather than fear will lead me to the answers I seek within or without.

My mind is open to receiving and using more of what has been made available to me from within or without. I can see potential answers to stressors in what previously seemed too new or unfamiliar. The Love, Life, and Energy God Is can be found in many more places and people than I had realized. The Gift of Creating Life will help me to develop new thoughts where older ones may not work or apply. I seek any who are willing to be my servant, and I theirs, while being the Love, Life, and Energy God Is. I am now the seeker of truth, human and Divine—and not only of the truth I want to know.

I now see conflict with my family, friends, and strangers in a different light. For so long, I had known conflict as a competition to be the representative of the truth—and I believed only I knew the real truth. I believed in an absolute truth with an attainable, consensual essence within the human realm for all manner of human disagreements. Now I recognize that this perception of truth was unrealistic due to the diversity of human nature. My goal of proving myself as keeper of the truth had often led me to disrespect my neighbors when they failed to agree with me. In doing so, I was failing to recognize that within any conflict, growth within the participants should be the real objective to be sought.

I have fully realized the harm I have done to others and myself within conflict. I had so often attempted to not only represent my truth, but to weaken or defeat others with it. I apologize to those who may not have been able to weather my attacks, Attacks which may have led them to feel less about themselves. These attacks may have unnecessarily led them away from their truth by overwhelming them with the conviction I had for my own. I understand now that I had recklessly dishonored them by failing to listen to their truth. I had also harmed myself with the demands I was placing upon others to know my truth. Demands in which I pushed away those who would be my friends. Demands in which I pushed away the very people who could teach and serve me. Demands in which I could have learned so much more than I was seeking to teach.

I now recognize how often fear rather than Love was guiding my thoughts within conflict. I felt afraid of not knowing the truth, and I often masked this fear with my insistence on knowing the truth for myself and everyone. By closing my mind and converting others to my truth, I worked to keep this fear at a distance. As I have awakened, I have realized that Love can be the only guide to the truth, either human or Divine. I no longer fear not knowing the truth. Earthly truth is to be sought within a shared journey. I am to be my neighbors' servant, and they mine. There is no greater service. Divine Truth has always been within me, ready to be known. I need only let it come forth while being the Love, Life, and Energy God Is and I Am.

CHAPTER 10

Higher Ego Flexibility Energy

Your Voice

I have learned to look for and know earthly and Divine Truth from within, not only from without. No longer do I disrespect my own thoughts and thinking. I no longer conclude that if my thinking is different than others, it must be wrong or I must conform my thoughts, values, or beliefs to those of others in order to know truth. I no longer need to fit my thinking into what others think or what I believe others want me to think. The errors that may appear within my thoughts are no longer seen as a reflection of my stupidity, but rather, as a reflection of my imperfection and humanity, for which I need make no apology. I also no longer neglect my better thoughts and ideas that work well for me, even if they don't work as well for others. I have become one of the right people to listen to.

Because of my newfound respect for my own thinking, I no longer give others a free pass into my mind. This faulty approach had been built upon my belief that they held ownership of the truth. I can see how oftentimes I was listening to the wrong people, at the wrong times, and about the wrong things—even if they meant well. I recognize how their version of earthly life and mine are different. Our difference often does not need to be reconciled and does not mean we disrespect one another if no reconciliation occurs. I also realize that those who cannot accept this or who would attempt to force their truth upon me are the wrong people for me to listen to. They are not being the Love, Life, and Energy God Is, as they do not truly seek to serve me, but themselves.

The weaknesses that may appear within my thinking no longer lead me to disown my mind and seek only the input of others. However, I strive to recognize when I truly am the wrong person to listen to, and I seek the counsel of others when necessary. I no longer fear the distance that may exist between faulty beliefs I may possess and truth, as this distance only reflects my human imperfection, to which I can respond by being the Love, Life, and Energy God Is and I Am. Divine Truth will assist me in my journey to human truth, allowing me to live the life I was meant to live.

I no longer become lost within the truth of my partner or other close loved ones. Previously, I had disappeared so fully into their beliefs, values, and thinking that I could no longer recognize myself. I no longer disrespect myself by needing to reconcile all of the differences within our respective human truths. A reconciliation built upon the illusion that abandonment of myself would bring greater love, closeness, and happiness to our relationship. I now realize that relationships are as much about respecting differences as they are about sharing commonalities, be they thoughts, interests, or activities.

I now also celebrate the healthy conflict that occurs within our relationship. A conflict in which I am now present and represented within our relationship, rather than remaining absent by adopting my partner's truth. By engaging in healthy conflict, I am gaining respect from my partner as I speak more of my own voice within our relationship. A respect I was denying to myself and partner in the living of one person's truth. Conflict has now interjected dynamism into our relationship, which can only exist when both partners are willing to teach and be taught while growing with and from each other.

Genuine communication, compromise, compassion, and creation are making their appearance within our relationship as well. None of these were truly available when I remained absent from it. I did not know who I was, and my partner could not recognize me either, as they were only looking into a mirror. I was present in body, but not mind or spirit. We now celebrate the fullness of a relationship that was hollow. Communication, compromise, compassion, and creation have filled in the hollow, now that I am contributing my thoughts and my truth, both human and Divine. I am no longer consumed with finding them within another to secure my safety and survival. This has allowed me to speak with my own voice in our relationship.

My love for myself is growing, as I have become true to myself. A truth in which I honor and respect my thoughts, be they weak or strong. No longer do I attach any conditions to truth with which to like or love myself. My thoughts reflect my human imperfection, an imperfection shared by all. I must work with my imperfection as I journey further and further into truth, both human and Divine. I have been given the wonderful gift of my mind with which to undertake this journey—a gift given in Love, and which I no longer neglect, as I now embody the Love, Life, and Energy God Is.

I therefore no longer refuse to know or accept my own thinking in order to like and love myself. I no longer require the truth of others to feel good about or accept myself. The illusion that I needed to do so was preventing me from loving and liking myself as I am. I no longer feel less about myself when my own truth does not overlap with that of my neighbor. Our truths express the diverse humanity we embody, not any inherent deficiencies beyond those of human imperfection. They need not be reconciled for either of us to love ourselves or one another.

I no longer allow others to force their truth upon me. I had so often permitted this because I believed that embracing the truth of others could allow me to experience greater love for myself. I had also made this allowance because I believed others would love me more for embracing their truth. Each of these ideas was an illusion, as love comes with neither of these conditions. I now realize that a righteous neighbor would never make this demand of me, nor would I need to ask it of them. A righteous neighbor would want me to stand upon my own truth and free to be me. A righteous neighbor would share his or her truth and honor mine, embodying the Love, Life, and Energy God Is.

My talents, interests, and potential are becoming fully known to me. I am finding them within my truth rather than seeking them within the truth of others—a truth which, even if well-intended, was often misguided and removed from the reality of who I Am. Others' truth often set me on the path of becoming what others would have me become, rather than myself. Their truth often made me feel lost, as if I were living the life someone else wanted for me. I realize that no one else can know the path I must take and the purpose I must serve, both human and Divine.

I no longer allow others or myself to judge me falsely. I now see how false judgments had often failed me with their ignorance of what was within me and around me in my efforts to achieve. So often I had let the wrong people or criteria judge me in ways that were ultimately unfair to me. So often I used the wrong references to judge how far I had come and how far I needed to go. I now act as my own reference point. A point of comparison built upon the truth of who I am within my abilities and interests. There can be no other reference point, as I can only be me, and only I can truly know what I can and should achieve. I use it while being the Love, Life, and Energy God Is and celebrating the gifts I have been given, both human and Divine.

As I have removed all of the untruths told by myself and others about my abilities, interests, and performance, I have come to believe in myself. Each of these untruths was a distortion and distraction from reality that could not serve my safety or survival. They could only serve as a false affirmation of my ability to gain protection within the truth of others. My belief in myself is rooted in the truth that I am doing the best I can do with what has been given to me. My life's work is empowered by human and Divine Truth. I no longer allow others or myself to stand in the way of this truth. I am far more empowered now, and I can offer greater service to others because I am living these truths.

I no longer believe in and seek an absolute human truth which exists in others. For so long I had entrusted ownership of my mind to others because of my belief that they held this truth. They were the ones I relied on to give me what I needed to know. They were the ones I wanted to change my thoughts where necessary. They were the ones whose thoughts I trusted to guide me in order to know a greater human truth. I relied on them in the illusion that they could only be the right people and I could only be the wrong person to change my thinking. A person whose different thoughts were only known to be deficient. The illusion that their thoughts were correct and mine were deficient has been shattered as I have come to know who I truly am and the gifts, both human and Divine, that I have been given. I am the owner of my mind and my truth, a truth both human and Divine that I seek from within and without. This search will allow me to live within my truth rather than survive within the truth of others.

My former illusions about the validity of my own thoughts had persisted for so long because I had been ignorant to the difference between belief and truth. This ignorance had made me naïve and gullible to the often faulty beliefs I readily learned from others in the name of truth. Others sometimes offered these beliefs to me with good intentions, while others acted maliciously. I am no longer blind as the difference is no longer hidden from me. Belief is no longer interpreted as a reflection of truth. Also, I no longer fear an absence of absolute human truth within myself that would lead me to search for it in others. An illusory search that was often intended to secure my survival. I am able to more closely look at belief in my journey to human truth without being taken in by it from within or without.

I now fully recognize my neighbors as well. I know that they were endowed with the same Divine Truth and Divine Gifts that I have been given. Like me, they can also become distanced from this awareness in their effort to survive with human truth alone. I also recognize my neighbors as having human imperfections like me. I know that in their imperfection, they may seek to serve themselves rather than me, and that whether or not they are fully aware of this, listening to them could at times weaken my mind if I do not think critically about their words. A service I can recognize in those who would seek to dishonor and replace my truth, human and Divine with their own. I no longer need to renounce my own mind in order to honor theirs. I can only respond to this service by being the Love, Life, and Energy God Is so they can better know their human and Divine Truth.

I no longer process the changes life brings mainly through the truth of another. My own thoughts, beliefs, and values serve as the filters through which I can understand the developmental, social, situational, and technological changes in my life. My own mind can best help me understand these changes and how to respond to them. I no longer respond to them only within the truth others have shown me. A truth which often worked better for who they were than who I am. I no longer allow others to own my response in the belief that it was based upon their truth and not my own. I own my own life and everything occurring within it. The gifts I have been given, human and Divine, allow me to take this ownership.

Change no longer poses the endangerment to my survival which I had known it to be. The endangerment truly resided in the illusory sense that I possessed a weakened mind unable to rely on its own thinking to understand and manage change. My progressive sense of weakness grew every time I asked others to think for me rather than thinking for myself. This weakness was intensified by the progressive distance I was gaining from my own truth, human and Divine. Now that I have awakened to both human and Divine Truth, I see change for what it truly is: an unfolding of energy along the path of life. An often positive and transformative energy calling upon my resources to manage it. An energy not to be feared when viewed with the light of my own truth, both human and Divine.

I now also recognize who the right and wrong people are to listen to in working with change. Friendship, good intentions, or conviction are no longer sufficient reasons to accept the guidance of others. Rather, I seek relevant experience and knowledge from within myself or those best qualified to provide guidance. I can listen to others when this is lacking within myself. Those who would seek to guide me toward my truth while being the Love, Life, and Energy God Is are neighbors I must listen to. They accept that I own my life, as I am the only one who can be responsible for it and live it.

The adversity which happens within my life is now being met within my own truth, both human and Divine. I no longer know my failures, losses, and mistakes within the truth of another. It is within my own thoughts and thinking that I understand the causes, responsibility, and solutions necessary for their management. I am guided from within rather than without unless I determine that I am the wrong person to provide myself with guidance in the moment at hand. The wisdom I am acquiring from within and without is allowing me to better know the sources of my difficulty and which solutions can address my needs.

I am no longer consumed by fear that my thoughts and mind cannot answer the problems I face. I no longer require the company of another's truth to do what I can do for myself when need be. I am now companied by my own truth and Divine Truth. These truths have empowered me to meet my challenges with the gifts I have been given, both human and Divine. Gifts I no longer neglect by resorting only to the truth of another. A truth which often did not know me or the life I am living. A truth which often asked me to look without rather than within. A truth which was often for the service of others and not myself.

The persons who can serve me within my weakness and times of need are better known. They do not ask me to believe unquestioningly in their own thoughts and beliefs. They do not insult or intimidate me if I seek to rest upon the use of my own mind in solving a problem. They do not place conditions upon our relationship within the acceptance of the truth they want me to know. Those who embody the Love, Life, and Energy God Is within their assistance are the ones I must listen to when needed. It is within their guidance that I move further into my truth, both human and Divine. They are strong enough to withstand my weakness and lift me up within my journey when I have fallen.

My emotion is no longer guided by the truth of another. A truth that often guided me to anger, fear, and sadness. Feelings born of my difficulty in separating belief from truth. Feelings born of believing too much in others and too little in myself. Feelings born of the illusion that what often worked for others would also work for me. Each of these neglecting the awareness that illusions of separation, unworthiness, and inequality could never lead to happiness within the truth of others. I am no longer separated, unworthy, and unequal within my truth, both human and Divine.

I had so desperately sought happiness within the truth of others where it could never be found. A desperation in which I often sought to live within the truth of others in order to feel the warmth of happiness. This illusory happiness came from without rather than within, where it must begin. I now realize that genuine happiness must come from within the knowledge of my truth, both human and Divine. A happiness coming forth from ownership and use of all of the gifts I have received, human and Divine. Happiness coming forth from my willingness to live rather than efforts to survive within the truth of another.

I no longer allow others to impact my feelings with free access to my mind. Particularly those who would seek to darken my feelings with their darker thoughts and faulty beliefs. I recognize them as only seeking to serve themselves, knowing they are not being the Love, Life, and Energy God Is. They are also recognized as being with their own darker emotions which they are knowingly or unknowingly attempting to instill within me. I will no longer accept their thoughts and feelings, as they are not born of my truth, human and Divine. I will seek to support them if they will give me their ear while being the Love, Life, and Energy God Is and I Am

I no longer see the stressors I am facing through the truth of others. Their truth had often led me to misunderstand stressors even if they offered me their truth with the best of intentions. A misunderstanding in which I often did not know the size of my stressor(s), their causes, how long I had been facing them, and how best to manage them. I have stopped relying on their judgment about stressors and started to hear more of what I need to hear from the right people, including myself when I am that person. I recognize that the right person to listen to possesses relevant experience and knowledge while being the Love, Life, and Energy God Is within their offering of wisdom.

I am also better able to know the stress I am experiencing. This recognition is no longer built upon biases, agendas, lack of objectivity, or flawed information offered by others, even those whose intentions are good. I am the person responsible for healing my mind and body, and I must do this with my own truth, human and Divine. It is within this truth that I can see what I must see, think what I must think, and do what I must do. Each has allowed me to manage my stress and stressors rather than letting them quietly manage me within the ignorance of both human and Divine truth.

As I have come to know my truth, the stress in my life and its sources have subsided. They are no longer fed by illusions of unworthiness, separation, and inequality about myself, which had served to empower them. They are no longer hidden or unmanageable within my truth, and they no longer seem larger or more frequent than they truly are. I had only made them so through the ignorance of my truth. My own imperfection and that of the human realm are readily manageable within the power of my truth, both human and Divine.

I have also come to recognize the importance of healthy conflict with my neighbors. I know that this experience can serve as a learning opportunity for each of us, catalyzing our personal growth. Healthy conflict can also honor my truth even as I seek to refine it. No longer do I view conflict as unnecessary, as challenging one another's beliefs can broaden our understanding. No longer do I see it as an opportunity for rejection by my neighbor due to my ignorance of my neighbor's truth. No longer do I view conflict as having only one potential winner, my neighbor.

I now honor my truth, both human and Divine. I honor it with my willingness to know and express it. I honor it with my willingness to recognize any error which exists within it and improve upon it where necessary. I honor it by not letting others prevent me from expressing it. Those who would deny me this opportunity are the wrong people with whom to be in conflict. They do not honor me or my truth, even though they are free to disagree with it. I can learn little or nothing from them, and they do not truly seek to serve me. They are not being the Love, Life, and Energy God Is.

I no longer listen to my neighbor in an unquestioning manner. I now display genuine skepticism and questioning in my encounters with them, rather than seeing these responses as signs of disrespect, which had previously led me to avoid conflict. I do not dishonor my neighbor with my disagreement and will not be disagreeable within its expression. Those who would hold me to account for my disagreement are the wrong people with whom to be in conflict. They do not seek to serve me, only themselves. I will no longer be taken in by them by dishonoring my truth in their presence. Those who are being the Love, Life, and Energy God Is would not ask this of me.

CHAPTER 11

Higher Ego Vulnerability Energy

Your Voice

I no longer see my neighbor through the lens of fear—a fear that often led me to hide from others or dominate them in my thoughts, words, and deeds. Thoughts, words, and deeds in which I sought to keep others at a distance from my weaknesses. Weakness if known by others would have made me weaker than I already thought myself to be. I no longer wear this mask, as I no longer fear my weakness. Human and Divine Truth have conquered my fear of my weakness. Weaknesses are a reflection of human imperfection known to all. It does not require an illusory removal to work and play with my neighbor. I can accept my weakness within the Divine Perfection of my being, and I no longer work in fear to hide or reject it in order to gain acceptance from my neighbors.

I no longer judge my neighbors unfairly with fear. A fear which often led me to fill in what I did not truly know about my neighbors. So often I had thought they were looking at me in a darkened way. I projected onto them negative thoughts about the way I appeared to them in my thoughts, words, and deeds. Often in error, as my fear did not allow me to truly know them. I now see they were usually neither judging me nor looking for my faults. These projections were born of my own deep illusions of unworthiness, separation, and inequality that I carried within. These illusions had prevented me from recognizing the Love, Life, and Energy God Is within my neighbor and myself. Divine Truth has now shed light on these illusions and freed me from them.

I no longer seek to defeat my neighbors as an affirmation of myself. A defeat in which I sought to make them weaker than me in their thoughts, words, and deeds. Any affirmation born of fear was only an illusion, as genuine affirmation can only exist within Love. I am sorry for any harm I have done to others within my fear, and I ask their forgiveness for my actions. I have learned what I have needed to learn, and I will affirm them as well as myself in Love.

My relationships with those closest to me are no longer seen through the lens of fear. For so long, fear had led me to distrust myself, my partner, or other close loved ones within our relationship. This distrust had often led me to unnecessarily question others to prove their love for me. In my distrust of them, I had also attempted to hide my weakness from them due to my fear of rejection or abandonment. My distrust led me to place myself above my partner and other loved ones so they would know their good fortune within our relationship. All of this distrust reflected an illusory relationship built upon fear, not Love. I now know that trust for myself or my partner can only exist within a truly loving relationship.

Due to my fear, I had often asked my partner or other loved ones to be my protector, someone I asked to answer the call of fear for me. I had mistreated them with anger when they did not answer my call. I will no longer ask them to be my protector, doing what I could do for myself. I thank them for their loyalty in the face of my fear, but I will no longer ask this of them. They have born the weight of my fear for too long, and I must remove it, using the weightlessness of Love to remove the heavy weight of fear. I feel genuine Love for myself and them, not a fear-based loyalty masquerading as Love. Divine Truth has shown me the way to this Love, which makes me want to embrace all that we can know in ourselves and our relationship. Far more than we have known exists within the abundance that has been made available to us, but I could not see it within my fear.

I am now able to serve my partner and loved ones within our relationship while being the Love, Life, and Energy God Is. For so long I have worn the neediness of fear and had not been serving them. I am now here for them to call upon within their time of need. I will be their rock if human darkness has befallen them. I am no longer absent in those times. Our relationship and gifts, human and Divine, will see us through those moments. We will answer every call together in Love, not within the darkness and isolation of fear.

I will raise myself up in Love, not fear, but not to be above or below others. I no longer ask others to love me when I could not love myself. The

Love God Is has taught me there can be no conditions from within or without to know Love for myself or others. I have learned that acceptance from others in the absence of self-acceptance is hollow. I no longer seek and require others to give me what is already inside me, the Love God Is. I need not love others in fear so I can know a hollow love from them or myself. I can give to myself in Love, no longer seeing it as selfish within the twisted notions of fear. Valuing others in fear cannot lead me to love myself. Love comes from within when being the Love God Is, rather than without. I therefore no longer seek to earn love. The illusions of unworthiness, separation, and inequality no longer exist to know myself in a darkness filled with fear.

I will no longer allow my human imperfection and my fear of it to guide my feelings about myself and my value of myself. This fear had often led me to know dishonor and shame for who I am, a person I did not truly know. A fear that often led me to seek to meet faulty conditions that would supposedly allow me to know honor and pride within myself. My fear often led me to ask others to love me, because I did not truly love myself. I no longer attach illusions of unworthiness, separation, and inequality to myself in a darkness filled with fear.

The Love God Is and I Am has taught me that there can be no conditions from within or without to know love for myself or others. I have learned that acceptance from others in the absence of my own is hollow. Thus, I no longer seek and require others to give what has already been given and is within me—the Love God Is. This Love is free and without burden. I need not love others in fear so I can know a hollow love for them or myself. Rather, I can give to myself in Love and no longer see this as selfish within the twisted notions of fear.

I raise myself up in Love, not fear. This empowering Love embraces my human imperfection even as I grow from and beyond it. It waters my soul, quenching its thirst. This Love has allowed me to truly know who I am, human and Divine. I no longer seek to rise above others or put others below me, as the Love God Is will not allow it. I can only be One and in Unity with my neighbors. My human imperfection cannot make it otherwise.

My expectations for and usage of my human gifts are no longer guided by fear and the need to remain at a distance from my imperfection. I no longer seek to refute my imperfection with my accomplishments. I no longer seek to know worthiness from my accomplishments. I no longer seek to have others honor me and know my worthiness from their acknowledgment of my accomplishments. Each of these desires is rooted in fear-based illusions of separation, unworthiness, and inequality—illusions that have led me to faultily use my talents in the service of fear-based needs. A service unto myself as one cannot offer true service to others in fear, only Love.

I no longer view with fear my competitors in the arena. As someone who would seek to remove the mask of my strength in order to reveal my weakness and imperfection. They are no longer the enemies I had known in fear but the neighbors I know in Love—neighbors who are seeking to honor their gifts and serve others with them just as I seek to do. I know them in the way God knows them. No longer do I seek to elevate myself above them in the illusion of gaining greater worthiness and importance through my accomplishments. My human and Divine Gifts were not given for this purpose. They can only be used while being the Love, Life, and Energy God Is. It is within this service that I can know my life's purpose and the greatest of accomplishments: entry into the Kingdom of Heaven.

I now view my talents, form my expectations, and recognize my achievements as well as those of others with Love, not fear. Fear had often led me to self-serving distortions that kept me from knowing my own weakness while knowing the weakness of my neighbors well. These distortions have been dissolved by Love, as in being the Love God Is, they can serve no purpose. There is no greater or lesser, more worthy or less worthy, more important or less important. Each is to be what they have been given. There are no comparisons to be made or standards to be reached when being the Love, Life, and Energy God Is. Each can only ask, "Am I being the Love, Life, and Energy God Is with what has been given to me?"

I have taken ownership of my mind in Love and not fear. So often I had questioned my thinking, leading me to ignore or attack my own thoughts. A neglect and attack of my own thoughts born of my need to limit their expression so as to hide my vulnerability and imperfection. I no longer seek to disown my mind, but to acknowledge and grow it both within and without. I no longer fear its weakness and imperfection, as these are part of my humanity. I no longer listen in fear to the thoughts of others to shield me from the weakness of my own mind. Rather, I seek to honor my mind with acknowledgement and expression.

I will not attack the mind of others in fear. In these attacks, I had challenged the thinking of others in order to establish a sense of superiority of intellect and mind. Now I realize that this effort was only an attempt to further distance me from the imperfection and weakness of my own mind.

My mind cannot be made greater, nor my imperfection lessened, by the illusory weakening of my neighbor's mind. I apologize to any whom I have harmed and dishonored with my assaults and insults upon their mind. These were truly reflections of my weakness and suffering born of fear. As with my mind, I will honor theirs in being the Love God Is.

I am able to think with my thinking rather than only with my emotion. No longer does fear guide me into unquestioned anxious or angry thoughts. I recognize that I have often created these thoughts in my fear, and that they were not a necessary response to what surrounded me. My mind has become sober in the absence of this fear—a sobriety in which objectivity, reflection, and deliberation have replaced subjectivity, impulsivity, and irrationality. Love now guides what must enter, be changed, or removed from my mind. It leads me to the human and Divine Truth upon which I can stand unafraid of the imperfection within my being and within the world.

I no longer insist on living in an unchanging world. Previously, I had insisted on not encountering change in my work, relationships, health, finances, or other aspects of life, due to fear of my weakness and vulnerability, from which I strove to remain at a distance. I no longer strive to always maintain consistency, familiarity, and predictability. They are no longer my only companions. They have been joined by the vibrancy, excitement, and challenge that change has to offer. Each has a place within my life while being the Love, Life, and Energy God Is—a life unknown to one living in fear and preoccupied with survival.

Thus, I no longer meet the changes that life brings to me with fear created by my own mind. A fear which sought to overcome the imperfection within my being. A fear which did not strengthen or protect me but only served to weaken me in the face of change. A fear which often led me to think many inaccurate thoughts about the change(s) before me. I had so often known changes as faster, larger, more unpredictable, and more unmanageable than they truly were. Fear had led me to magnify them in the interest of my safety and survival—an unnecessary enlargement that had only led me into suffering.

I now embrace change with Love and not fear, calling upon my own sober thoughts to know and manage it. I call upon human and Divine Truth rather than untruth in working with change. Furthermore, I recognize that change can often be a friend contributing to my growth, rather than an enemy seeking my defeat by exposing my imperfection and vulnerability. I no longer seek to disown this human vulnerability within the mindlessness of fear. Rather, I honor my vulnerability by using the gifts I have been given, human and Divine, to manage the changes life brings to me.

The adversity I am facing in life is no longer seen through the lens of fear. This fear had often led me to hide my mistakes, losses, and failures from myself or others, an attempt to keep myself and others at distance from my vulnerability. An unnecessary distance when one comes to know oneself in Love and not fear. I no longer seek to avoid, ignore, or overcome my vulnerability. I embrace the errors within my humanity in Love, rather than rejecting them in fear. Within this Love, I seek to learn and grow from my errors so I can better serve myself and others while being the Love, Life, and Energy God Is.

I also no longer view my neighbors with fear and its companion, anger, no longer seeing my neighbors as people who would prey upon and celebrate my weakness. I now know that most people do not seek to lower me by exposing my weakness to others, or place themselves above me with the knowledge of my weakness. Each of these ideas is an invention of my fear born in the illusions of separation, unworthiness, and inequality. Those who are being the Love, Life, and Energy God Is would never seek to do me harm because of my weakness. For those who would seek to do me harm, I can only answer them in Divine Truth and serve them within their weakness if called.

I no longer renounce my vulnerability by seeking to become invulnerable. An invulnerability in which my failures, losses, and mistakes were rejected. A rejection in which I found the roots to their occurrence within the weakness of others and life. Weakness within their thoughts, words, deeds, and circumstances they were required by me to own. An ownership that isolated and insulated me from an awareness of my own weakness and vulnerability. Through the human and Divine Truth to which I have awakened, I now recognize the illusion of my invulnerability. The empowerment these truths have imparted to me has allowed me to release the illusion of my invulnerability and human perfection.

The emotions of anxiety, anger, depression, and pseudo-happiness have all subsided as well. Each of these emotions was rooted in fear—a fear that led me to use thoughts, words, and deeds linked to these emotions in the name of my safety and survival. I have learned that my safety and survival was already ensured by human and Divine Truth. I have also learned that fear can only distance me from my truth, human and Divine, not allow me to know it. Fear can only lead me into unnecessary suffering, not deliver me from it. Fear has been my true enemy, and not, as you would have me believe, my friend.

You had led me to believe that my happiness could be known by the distance I had gained from my human vulnerability. I now recognize this belief as a renouncement of myself in which no happiness could truly lie. There can be no happiness within ignorance or rejection of myself, only suffering, misery, and an illusory chase for something that cannot exist under the conditions I had placed upon it. My rejection of the illusions of separation, inequality, and unworthiness have eliminated my fear of my vulnerability, opening the door to knowing genuine happiness within my truth, human and Divine, and the recognition of the Divine Gifts I have been given.

Due to these revelations, I will no longer use the human gifts of my emotions as tools rooted in fear, but rather, in compassion for myself and others. They must play their part in guiding me to healthier reality-based thoughts, words, and deeds. I will no longer drown within my emotions or fear them as a reflection of my vulnerability. They are here to assist me as I embrace my humanity and Divinity.

I no longer view stressors in my life through the lens of fear. This fear had often made larger what was smaller, more frequent what was less frequent, and unmanageable what was manageable within the illusory service of my safety and survival. This did not truly serve me, but led me into great suffering, which I had known in the form of fear-based thoughts, words, and deeds intended to protect me and ensure my survival. I now recognize the harm I had done to myself and others through this suffering.

My mind, body, and emotions now work in concert to address the stressors I face. No longer do my feelings and bodily symptoms lead me into fearful thoughts and behaviors. I no longer readily enter into and remain within them. I am no longer consumed and distracted by them in ways that had led me to exist without really living. My mind and body are no longer imprisoned by fear and the need to distance myself from my human vulnerability. Human and Divine Truth have freed me from the prison of fear. Reality-based thoughts and the Love, Life, and Energy God Is and I Am have empowered me to answer any of the challenges I may face.

The body I have been given is no longer worn with stress. I had been asking it to frequently warn me of danger when no true danger existed. I now ask it to warn me only when necessary. Within a reality-based life, there is no need to hide in fear from healthy human vulnerability and the stressors that one may encounter. I honor and care for my body in human and Divine Truth so I can fully know this gift, which I am meant to use in service to myself and others rather than scorning it with suffering rooted in fear.

Fear no longer dominates me when I experience conflict with my neighbor. It does not lead the shaping of my thoughts, words, or deeds. I no longer withdraw from or unnecessarily attack my friends, family, or strangers in order to ensure my survival. My thoughts are more sober and I do not seek to gain victory or avoid defeat within them. There can be no victory unless it is shared while being the Love, Life, and Energy God Is. Victory is no longer necessary to confirm illusions of unworthiness, separation, or inequality in myself or my neighbors. Defeat is unknown within Divine Truth, as there can be no greater or lesser than, only Oneness and Unity. Conflict can no longer separate me from my neighbor to ensure my survival.

I no longer fear conflict as an opportunity to expose my vulnerability to myself or others. The acknowledgment of my weakness and imperfection has allowed me to work with it rather than hide it. It is not a stain to remove or deny, but a place to grow from in a journey of never-ending growth within the human realm. I know that I need not fear this journey. Fear no longer drives me to seek perfection or hide the imperfection within my humanity. This companion has been replaced by Love, which helps me to know the imperfection of my humanity and the Perfection of my Divinity. Conflict is but an exercise for coming to know the former, and I embrace it with Love rather than fear.

I apologize to those with whom I have entered into conflict with fear. A fear in which I had brought pain and suffering to others in the denial of my vulnerability and the need to ensure my survival through victory. I was not being the Love, Life, and Energy God Is within those moments. I have overcome that ignorance, and I see light where there had been darkness. I ask these others to serve me and allow me to serve them as we journey forth in Divine Truth to enter the Kingdom of Heaven along the paths we each must take.

CHAPTER 12

Lower Ego Vulnerability Energy

Your Voice

I no longer keep distance from my emotion in the company of my neighbors. No longer do I see emotion as an enemy attempting to expose my vulnerability to myself or others. Rather, I now know it as a human gift that allows me to feel passion within my thoughts, words, and deeds as I undertake my life's work. This human gift allows me to feel compassion for myself and others in our time of need. It also serves to guide me to better thoughts, words, and deeds as I healthfully manage the imperfection of my humanity. Within my emotion I have the ability to fully embrace my humanity and make whole what was hollow. Through this wholeness, I have awakened to each of the Divine Gifts I have received.

The wall between my neighbors and me has been torn down. This wall built with the absence of emotion. It was behind this wall that I did not have to know them nor allow them to know me. A wall in which I could keep them in ignorance of my weakness and vulnerability. A wall in which I could live in the denial of my weakness, need not own it, or be obligated to others for it. I now realize that all of this was an illusion. I could not truly hide from my neighbors, as there was no wall that kept them from seeing me. They could see me better within their human and Divine Truth than I could see myself within my untruth. I now see how they often stood by me in my darkness, and I thank them for their service to me.

Emotion is no longer a tool to be used for my amusement, pleasure, or alleviation of boredom. Abuse and misuse of it had often led to pain and suffering for myself and others. Each thought, word, or deed born of emotional contrivance only served to distance me from my humanity and Divinity. I apologize to those I had preyed upon within my time of darkness. I will now serve them and myself within the joy and happiness of being the Love God Is. Within this Love, all of the human emotions I know will be honored in service to all.

I no longer remain at an emotional distance from my partner or close loved ones. Though I had been physically and mentally present, I have often been emotionally absent. An absence built upon the illusory notion that I was being strong when I was really keeping distance from my weakness, imperfection, and vulnerability. This distance had led me to refuse my partner's warm embraces, loving words, and kind gestures. I no longer view displaying these loving behaviors as signs of weakness. They are now known as opportunities to reveal my human truth and reflections of strength— the strength of Oneness and Unity that comes with acknowledging and expressing my feelings and baring my soul.

I apologize to my partner for my emotional absence in our relationship. For so long I had ignored or rebuffed my partner's attempts to get closer to me. I made hollow the warm embraces, loving words, and kind gestures my partner tried to give me. I was afraid that I would be opened up and that my partner would see all of who I am, including my weakness and vulnerability. I now see that my partner was leading me to what I truly needed—the need to know my human vulnerability rather than run from it. I now see my partner was being strong, embracing rather than fearing human imperfection, while I was being weak. They did not have the fear of their humanity that I had known for mine.

The emotion I did permit myself to experience and express was born of contrivance. A contrivance in which I set the terms for any feelings, be they love, anger, or fear, being shown. Contriving my emotions so carefully led me to feel safe, rather than permitting myself to be led into the unknown by my feelings. This contrivance also allowed me to experience the arousal, stimulation, and pleasure of my emotions without the risk of entering into the unknown. I now recognize the disingenuousness of this contrivance and its purpose in keeping me distant from my partner. I did not want to need or feel obligated to my partner, and maintaining this distance allowed me to refrain from feeling this obligation. I now see that this pattern was rooted in the fear of my vulnerability, a fear that could not exist in the confines of a genuine relationship. This fear no longer exists, as I have entered the realm of human and Divine Truth.

I no longer allow the absence of emotion to keep me at a distance from truly knowing myself. An absence in which I could be falsely strengthened by the ignorance of my weakness and the true nature of my vulnerability. Weakness and vulnerability others could more readily see. I am no longer in hiding from myself, and no longer do I know myself as invulnerable. My emotion has led me to know who I truly am, and I no longer fear getting to know the person I am. Human and Divine Truth have allowed me to make friends with this person—a person who is no greater or lesser than others, as the recognition of these truths reveals.

My human gift of emotion has also allowed me to genuinely celebrate my neighbors. I am able to truly recognize and acknowledge their attributes and accomplishments, rather than displaying the indifference and detachment I had often shown. I have learned that within human and Divine Truth, one can only be elevated when one's neighbors have been elevated, and never above them. Elevating myself above my neighbor was only an illusion, as I had actually been lowering myself. It is within those times, that I was not being the Love, Life, and Energy God Is and I Am.

My emotion now allows me to hear my neighbors. I am no longer deaf to the weakness and vulnerability they may call to my attention, and I no longer hear them with indifference and detachment. Rather, I now honor their thoughts and work with them to grow within my human weakness and vulnerability. I recognize them as offering service to me, a service I was unable to render to myself due to my emotional isolation. I now thank them where once I ignored or scorned them for calling attention to my weakness and vulnerability.

My emotions have opened doors to the use of all of my abilities which were previously closed. No longer do I neglect my potential if an activity does not give me immediate pleasure. No longer do I stop doing something early on if I meet with frustration or failure. No longer do I determine the meaning and importance of doing something by the pleasure it can give to me. My emotions have allowed me to become more patient and deliberate so that all of my interests and talents can be revealed to me.

I have become an honest judge of myself. My emotions have allowed me to see more of what has been done and left undone. Through them, I am better able to see what has been done well and less well, rather than overestimating my successes and overlooking my failures. I have become more accountable to myself and others. My emotions have also allowed me to recognize more of the talents and successes of my neighbors than I had known. I can now genuinely celebrate their successes and achievement rather than minimizing them with detachment and indifference.

I am now able to work with my interests and abilities in the service of others, not only myself. My emotions have allowed me to better know the needs of others and how I can use what I have to offer to serve them as well as myself. I am no longer selfish, and I seek to share the human and Divine Gifts I have been given. My emotions have delivered me from the emptiness of pleasure into the joy and happiness of service—a service which is of the highest calling and meaning.

My emotions are now a participant within the shaping of my thinking. Love, anxiety, anger, sadness, and guilt now help me better recognize the weakness, imperfection, and vulnerability within my thoughts and myself. It is within these emotions that I can consider the beliefs, values, and knowledge existent within my mind. These emotions have allowed me to question more deeply what must be questioned within my mind. These emotions are now available within the efforts I am making to grow my mind. Efforts which involve adding, changing, or removing that which is needed or unneeded.

I no longer view emotion as a threat to the effectiveness of my thinking and the intelligence of my thoughts. Emotions are not an enemy to my thoughts, but an aide. I now know them as gifts that can lead me closer to my human and Divine Truth. No longer do I seek these truths with a purely objective, logical, and emotionless mind. The truth does not reside there as this neglects the totality of my being and the life that surrounds me. It is like space without air in it. There can be no complete grasp of life without the emotion contained within it and me. The weakness in my thinking was not within the presence of emotion but within its absence. The presence of emotion can help me to learn more of what I need to think rather than what I want to think.

I apologize to those with whom I have been insensitive, disrespectful, and reckless in the expression of my thoughts and the reception of theirs. I no longer only see the strength within mine or the weakness within theirs. My emotion has allowed me to narrow the distance between us. It has removed the fear of my imperfection and the weakness within my thoughts. Illusions of sensing all energy, invisibility, and egoic control no longer blind me to all that is transpiring within and around me. These illusions had led me to insist upon having a rational, objective, and fully knowable human world built from the workings of my own mind—a world that would ultimately protect me and ensure my survival. I now realize no such world exists or needs to exist. I am now open to learning from others what I cannot learn from myself, an opportunity to be the Love, Life, and Energy God Is using the human and Divine Gifts we have all been given.

My emotions have awakened me to all of the changes occurring within and around me, allowing me to appropriately manage and learn from them. Change which I had been missing, neglecting, overlooking, or ignoring which needed my attention. Love, anxiety, anger, guilt, and sadness have led me to notice more of the interpersonal, developmental, health-related, financial, and situational changes unfolding before me. I am more connected to these changes and own my responsibility in working with them. No longer do I see myself as immune to or unreachable by the changes in my life—an idea that was only the illusion of my emotionless mind that served to distance me from my weakness, imperfection, and vulnerability.

I no longer instigate change as a way to avoid or remove boredom in my life, whether involving jobs, relationships, residences, or pastimes when they were no longer fun or gave me pleasure. Often I had abandoned them too soon, before I had given myself and them the opportunity they deserved. I had sought change for the sake of temporarily knowing excitement, arousal, and stimulation before boredom and stillness set in, signaling need for the next change. I now realize the stillness was within—a stillness no external change could ever diminish. Being emotionally present has removed this stillness and replaced it with passion, which has allowed me to know the excitement, arousal, and stimulation of meaning within my life. I now derive meaning from where, what, and whom I am within my life, allowing me to know happiness rather than just pleasure within my life.

I apologize to those I had often abandoned or abruptly left behind. I often misled and misused them for my enjoyment and pleasure. They gave me an opportunity for work or a relationship, but I could not stay. The stillness within me could not tolerate it. This was the basis for my betrayal of their efforts and goodwill. I could not welcome them with the depth and meaning of emotion that was required. I could only be shallow and superficial which made it easy for me to move on to the next change. My leaving was not of their doing, but my own. I hope they are receiving what they were looking for and deserve, both within and without.

My emotions are now allowing me to see what I could not see in their absence. My ignorance of my failures, losses, and mistakes did not mean they were not occurring. There is no protection or survival in the illusion that they were not taking place, only ignorance—an ignorance of my weakness and vulnerability, which could not serve me well. I no longer need to survive within this ignorance, as emotions have allowed me to know my human and Divine Truth.

The emotions of love, anxiety, anger, guilt, and sadness have awakened me to my failings. They have allowed me to see more of—and fully own— what I have done to myself and others within my weakness and imperfection. They have allowed me to respond with sober thoughts, words, and deeds to what I have done to myself and others. The gift of my emotion has allowed me to fully know and own my humanity. Emotions have brought light where there was darkness. I now know that there is no darkness I must run from or avoid in the name of my safety and survival within the Kingdom of Heaven.

I apologize to those I have harmed in the absence of my emotion. I can now see the insensitive, inconsiderate, and reckless thoughts, words, or deeds I had sent their way when I was asleep—a slumber in which I could not fully recognize the depth of my weakness and imperfection. They and I are worthy of so much more when being the Love, Life, and Energy God Is. My awakening will bring them the kindness, respect, and sensitivity they deserve as I make my way along the rest of my journey.

Through these changes, I have awakened from the imprisonment of my emotional absence. I once believed this prison freed me from the dangers of emotional entanglement and obligation. However, this "freedom" only brought me emptiness and a weakened sense of purpose and meaning within my life. A freedom which often had me seeking the pleasure of emotion on my terms. A freedom in which I could feel love, fear, guilt, anger, or sadness when I wanted to feel it and not when I needed to feel it. My awakening has allowed me to follow my emotions rather than leading them. I am no longer suspicious of them, and I welcome them when they lead me to my weakness, imperfection, and vulnerability. These emotional gifts have freed me to know my human and Divine Truth.

Awakening to my emotions has given me the opportunity to know genuine love and happiness. One cannot love others from a distance, as with Love there is connection, Oneness, and Unity. One does not orchestrate the manifestation of love, as with Love there are no boundaries or conditions. One does not fear Love, as these emotions are incompatible. Happiness can only be known when one is at peace with oneself, others, and the world. I know that I can experience happiness by working with my emotional gifts to reconcile and unite the imperfection of my humanity with the Perfection of my Divinity.

I apologize to myself for being emotionally absent in my own life. I have missed so much of myself, others, and life within this absence. My emotional detachment has often muted my awareness of the vibrancy and meaning playing out in the life before me. I was emotionally unavailable and could not be touched by emotion in ways that would have served me. Often others, be they animals, plants, or humans, were being the Love, Life, and Energy God Is, but I could not see it within their thoughts, words, and deeds. I could not fully embrace the Gifts of Life and Creating Life or witness them in others within my emotional absence. My awakening has brought all of this into focus. I can now celebrate in joy and happiness all that has been given in Love to me.

I am no longer removed from the stressors occurring within my life by the absence of emotion. Emotional warning bells are now sounding to bring my attention to what must be addressed within and around me. Be they health, interpersonal, financial, or other life-related stressors. I will no longer ignore, overlook, or minimize them, but will give them the attention they deserve. An attention in which I can be of greater service to others and myself within more appropriate thoughts, words, and deeds than were available within the absence of my emotion.

My emotions have taught me that I was not as immune to my stressors as I had believed myself to be. Their impact was being manifested in stressful thoughts, behaviors, and physical symptoms disconnected from the anger and fear that was welling from within. I was under attack but did not know it. I lived within the illusions of immunity and invincibility, as I could not feel the emotion I needed to feel in order to know my imperfection and vulnerability. These illusions have been removed with the friendship of my emotion which has allowed me to directly face the challenges that enter my life. A friendship in which my mind and body are no longer at a distance from each other, but are connected through the emotion and Love I have come to know.

I apologize to those to whom I have been a stressor and brought stress into their life. I now see how often I had precipitated anger or fear within them with my thoughts, words, and deeds, which often were not about them but for my own pleasure. I orchestrated them so I would feel something when I could feel nothing, seeking an opportunity to enjoy emotional arousal and stimulation that came at others' expense. I was manipulating emotion and others for my enjoyment and pleasure. They were innocent victims of my desires, though I did not recognize this at the time. I wish them well and hope they are healed from the exploitation and victimization I had brought to their door. I also apologize to those with whom I had been oblivious to the stress I had caused you within the absence of my emotion. I now recognize the callous, reckless, and insensitive thoughts, words, and deeds I used were often the source of distress and discomfort for you unseen by my emotional absence.

The conflicts with my neighbor are now becoming fully recognized. My emotion has taught me more about the frequency, depth, and impact they have had upon others than I had realized. I have been involved in more conflicts with my neighbors than my emotionless existence had led me to know. I have often hurt them more deeply and for longer than I knew. I apologize for the often uncaring, insensitive, and detached manner with which I treated them during our moments of conflict. I now honor and respect them at all times while being the Love, Life, and Energy God Is.

I can now learn from conflict what I was unable to learn before. My emotions have allowed me to hear more of what I need to hear, rather than only what I want to hear. They are allowing me to recognize more of my weakness and vulnerability as well. I no longer remain at a comfortable emotionless distance from them, which had only served to make me weaker, not stronger. This distance had removed me not only from my human truth but also from my Divine Truth. My emotion has eliminated this distance, and I am free to learn everything I must learn on my journey to the Kingdom of Heaven.

Conflict will no longer be a tool for my amusement. In the past, I had precipitated conflict to experience the excitement, arousal, and pleasure that experiencing emotion can bring. I was seeking conflict for conflict's sake, not to genuinely learn or teach anything with it. This was a betrayal of the human gift of my emotion, in which I used this gift simply for the pleasure it could give me. It was also a betrayal of those with whom I was in conflict who did not recognize its true purpose for me. These betrayals can no longer take place within my awakening to my human and Divine Truth. I now celebrate my emotions with understanding of the true purpose for which they were given—to be the Love, Life, and Energy God Is as I move forward on my journey to the Kingdom of Heaven.

THE TRANSCENDENCE

One Voice

The awakening to the Two Voices of Ego and Spirit and transformation into the speaking of your voice has led you into Egospiritualism. Within this egospiritualistic consciousness, you have reconciled the imperfection of your humanity and the Perfection of your Divinity. No longer are you ignorant of them or know them as opposing forces. No longer do you seek what cannot be found within your humanity to fill the void of your unrecognized Divinity. No longer do you wander in the darkness of your humanity on an aimless journey seeking and hoping for the best an earthly life can offer. You have learned what must be learned and unlearned what is illusion as you have come to listen to both Ego and Spirit and to speaking your own voice. The merging of your humanity and Divinity has led you to One Voice. A voice in concert with the universe.

You have entered into the light of a consciousness in which you recognize your connection to all that was, is, and will be—a connection to all beings in Oneness and Unity. Within this consciousness, the words "unworthy," "unequal," and "separate" have no meaning. There is no meaning to the words "past" or "future." The words "you" and "they," "here" and "there," also have no meaning. Human meanings such as these have no place within

Divine Truth. This consciousness allows you to see well beyond the boundaries of your human senses and thoughts, fully recognizing the workings of Divine Truth and allowing all to be fully known.

As the One Voice is spoken within Egospiritualism the sequential process of Awakening, Transformation, and Transcendence accelerates into simultaneous occurrence. Each begin occurring at the same time as the vibrational frequency increases moving one forward into progressively higher levels of spiritual consciousness. A consciousness in which Spirit moves further and further into the foreground of your consciousness while Ego moves further and further into the background until you have returned home to the Kingdom of Heaven when Ego will no longer exist in the absence of its purpose to help you to survive. Its loving service has ended as survival has no place within the Kingdom of Heaven. It is within the complete dissolution of your Ego that you are fully transformed, fully transcendent, and fully enter the Kingdom of Heaven.

The One Voice is a universal melody sounding from within and without. A melody to be thought, spoken, and lived by all who are entering into the Kingdom of Heaven. This melody is the Voice of God.

One Voice spoken only in peace.
One Voice spoken only in love.
One Voice spoken with joy and happiness.
One Voice spoken in respect of the body, mind, and spirit.
One Voice spoken in honor of all earthly gifts received.
One Voice spoken with healthy expectations for all.
One Voice spoken in morality guided by healthiness.
One Voice spoken here, now, and always.
One Voice spoken in connection to all beings
from all times and all places.
One Voice spoken within the Divine Gifts all have been given.
One Voice spoken in Divine Truth.
One Voice spoken to guide all on their
journey to the Kingdom of Heaven.

CHAPTER 13

The Divine Truth

God Is Love

The One Voice is spoken in Love. A voice now heard within falling rain, the warm rays of the sun, and the blowing of the wind. A voice now heard within the illumination of light, the beauty of sound, the breathing of air, and the warmth of touch. A voice now heard in soothing words, kind thoughts, and the comfort offered by a neighbor. It is an unbounded, unlimited, unburdened, and connective Love available to all within their Divinity. A Love from which you can no longer gain distance, as you have awakened to Divine Truth.

A Love without person, place, or time. It can only be and cannot be. There is no beginning or end to this Love. These are only distinctions made by those who have not yet awakened. There is no right person to find or not find it within, as all persons are connected as One within it. There is no place to find or not find it, as all places are connected as One within it. There is no time for it, as it is timeless. It is within all times, good or bad, happy or sad. Illusions of person, place, or time built upon the imperfection of humanity can no longer conceal the Love God Is.

A Love with unlimited supply and power available for all to use. It knows no human challenge it cannot meet as they are made weak by it. It knows no time in which to call upon it, as it is available at all times. The only time it can be is within this time, as it knows no past or future. It knows no fear which it cannot remove as it is beyond the fear created within the human realm. It contains the empowerment of Oneness and Unity to defeat the isolation and separation of fear. A fear which received its faulty empowerment within earthly illusions. Illusions readily removed by this Love which speaks Divine Truth.

A Love without burden and which is weightless. It requires no effort, as it defies the conditions of the human realm. There is no giving or receiving within the Divine Realm, only being. This Love can only be "given" or "received" freely when being the Love God Is. One cannot ask for or earn what is already within one's being. Earthly thoughts, words, and deeds are offered in being the Love God Is. There need be no acknowledgement, celebration, or debt attached to them. These are only human requirements placed upon love within the earthly realm. When being the Love God Is, there can be no other way. When transcending into the Divine Realm, one can only be the Love God Is.

A Love which is connective, allowing one to know all that is available in the human and Divine Realms. It speaks to your connection to all beings from all places and all times within the Unity and Oneness of the Kingdom of Heaven. It carries all who have chosen to awaken to it forward within the connection of their body, mind, and spirit. A Love connecting you to each of the Divine Gifts which have been given. Within this Love, fear has no place to separate you from all that has been given for you to enter the Kingdom of Heaven.

God Is Life

The One Voice is spoken in Life. A voice in which the presence of God is known in all living things. A voice in which there can be no beginning or end to life, only transformation and transcendence. A voice in which there is only being as one witnesses life. All life is honored without distinction within this voice. It fully reveals the Life God Is, which can no longer remain unrecognized within human imperfection and illusions. The darkness within your humanity can no longer keep you at a distance from the Life God Is, within and without.

There is no longer a search for the presence of God. It is within and all around you. You find it within the nearest or most distant person, animal, insect, or plant. You know God is there because as with you it could not be without the Life God Is within it. You can celebrate the accompaniment of God which has always been. An accompaniment in which you are always *walking in the presence of God wherever you find life or wherever life finds you.*

When hearing this voice, there is no longer concern or fear about the ending of your earthly life. The Life God Is lies beyond one's mortality. It is a life of transformation and transcendence—a movement of one's soul along the path to the Kingdom of Heaven. One can never be fully removed from connection with loved ones past, present, or future by earthly death. The Life God Is lies beyond this earthly limitation.

The Life God Is, is without punishment, here or beyond. You need not fear punishment from God, now or then. Your suffering and punishment was born of your own making when choosing to live beneath human and Divine Truth. The hell you may envision is only of your earthly making. It has no place within the awareness that God Is Life. You need not make your peace with God, only yourself, as God has always "known" and "understood" your weakness better than you. There is only further transformation and transcendence to be known in the Life God Is.

The Life God Is can be known by being within the here and now, through a deep connection to what is occurring within your thoughts, feelings, and behaviors. It is not diluted by consumption with the past or concerns about the future in this moment or any moment. Time is no longer a relevant awareness, as before and after serve no purpose. There are only a series of "now" moments upon which notions of the past and future are known. The lifeless mixture of the past with the present and the present with the future have been replaced by the "lifeful" moments of the present. The Life God Is fully empowers these experiences, connecting you to all that you encounter.

The Life God Is, is fully honored. You know each representation of this Life in dignity. A dignity in which there is no questioning of presentation or purpose of the life form you are beholding. You no longer see the differences between life forms through notions of separation, inequality, or unworthiness. The mysteries of life no longer require understanding and justification to accord them with honor and dignity. Faith and trust in the Life God Is, is all that is necessary until the moment of revelation.

God Is Energy

The One Voice is spoken in Energy. An Energy which empowers the Light and Truth existent within all that life is. An Energy giving movement and dynamism through the positive transformation it sets forth within all beings. *An Energy which can heal all from within as its essence is Truth. This Energy was, is, and will always be.*

The Energy God Is brings forth Light and Truth to all who seek to know it. It lifts darkness for any who are in darkness within their thoughts, words, and deeds and removes the untruth that created the darkness. Darkness cannot remain within the presence of this Energy. This Energy illuminates all that has been made available within the earthly and Divine Realms. Darkness will never be known again within the awareness of the Energy God Is.

The Energy God Is brings forth growth and transformation. Transformation built upon truth, human and Divine. A movement in which one can only move forward when one has become revealed to oneself. It is within this Energy that all is made available to all. An Energy not of the past or the future, but of now. An Energy which cannot be encased in time as this violates its essence. An Energy in which personal and collective evolution occurs in the journey to the Kingdom of Heaven.

The Energy God Is allows for all healing. It is not bounded by person, place, or time for this healing to occur. A healing from within that is available to all. One need only choose oneself to know this healing. Seek it from within, where it awaits in all times and all places. Within this Energy, one is set free from any earthly obstacles in the journey to the Kingdom of Heaven.

The Energy God Is has and will always be spoken in One Voice.

God Is You

The One Voice is spoken within You. You are the coalescence of the Love, Life, and Energy God Is within your being. Its sounds resonate in the thoughts, words, and deeds of Unity and Oneness coming forth from within your being and all beings. This loud and relentless voice calls forth from within and without. It is a voice of Love and Peace fully heard and spoken without earthly boundaries. A voice announcing each of the Divine Gifts that all have received.

Through this voice, you have come to know and own the Gift of Life. A Gift in which you have entered the center of your life and are not allowing your life to be defined by what surrounds it. You awaken each day with the awareness that each breath drawn, melody heard, movement taken, and dream envisioned are reflections of the opportunity given to be the Life God

Is. Whatever you took for granted, be it large or small, now has meaning. Your being has taken on a meaning and purpose previously unknown to you. You are no longer here simply because you are here. You are here to be the Love, Life, and Energy God Is within your choosing. A choice of your own making which can only be made by you. A choice with no possible error when being the Love, Life, and Energy God Is. You have chosen yourself.

This voice has also allowed you to know and own the Gift of Creating Life. You are the creation of your own creation. The endowment of your human gifts has been made fully known to you. As you work with them, they take you to a greater place than you had known—a place you can only know when creating with your own thoughts, words, and deeds. You can only arrive at this place when being the Love, Life, and Energy God Is within your creations. A place amongst many along your journey to the Kingdom of Heaven.

You have come to know and own the Gift of Eternal Life. Your earthly need to survive and fear of death have been removed and replaced by an awakening to your immortality. You are a being without beginning or end, birth or death, within the Divine Realm. Your being supersedes the boundaries of the earthly realm, as you are the Love, Life, and Energy God Is. Through this Gift, you are freed to undertake your earthly work without the unnecessary distractions of your health, age, or mortality. Each day is to be celebrated within your youth or maturity, as a never-ending series of "nows." Your life's work is on "Divine Time," and there is no concern about its completion within your earthly life and earthly time.

You have come to know and own the Gift of God Within, a companionship from which you can never be separated or walk alone, as you are the Love, Life, and Energy God Is. Within this Unity and Oneness, you are guided and accompanied along your journey to the Kingdom of Heaven. Your journey's length is to be determined by you, but the destination is the same for all—the Kingdom of Heaven.

AFTERWORD

"Go in Peace to Serve the Lord!"

A message heard weekly by millions of people at the close of a religious service. A profound message often underappreciated in the midst of preparations for leaving the house of worship, thoughts about the day's subsequent activities, or its mere repetition contributing to a sense of numbness to its depth of meaning. An unfortunate lack of awareness missing the profound essence contained within seven words. Possibly, the most important words of the entire service offering a plan for the living of one's life. A message to be carried forth serving as the shepherd to we who are the lambs.

We are being told to go forth from this place within or without. To move forward along our journey to whomever, wherever, and whatever we must do to walk our path into the Kingdom of Heaven.

We are being told our journey can only be one of peace. A journey in which all that we encounter must be met with peace. Otherwise, the journey will be met with darkness and delay our entry into the Kingdom of Heaven.

We are being told our purpose for being is to serve and that the highest calling is to be that of servant. A service to all offered in Divine Truth and with all of the gifts, earthly and Divine, that we have been given. A service leading us to the Kingdom of Heaven.

We are being told to honor the Lord in any way which is in keeping with one's tradition and to respect those of our neighbors. Be the Lord—Yahweh, Allah, the Great Spirit, Source, One's Higher Power, Vishnu, or God.

10360101R00129

Printed in Great Britain
by Amazon.co.uk, Ltd.,
Marston Gate.